Praise for Not Your Parents' Workplace

"This book is far more than one man's journey through the pressure-filled halls of Wall Street and into the heart of Silicon Valley. Nathan Tanner has extracted hard-won lessons from his own experience and created a practical, relevant guide to help all newcomers get into the game and thrive in the new world of work."

–Liz Wiseman, Bestselling author of *Multipliers* and *Rookie Smarts*

"*Not Your Parents' Workplace* is an insightful and candid look at the new career landscape. You'll learn a lot from Nathan's journey. Better yet, you'll be inspired by his hustle and persistence."

–Ben Casnocha, Co-author of #1 New York Times bestseller *The Start-up of You*

"Nathan Tanner's insights on career choices reflect wisdom personified. He has extracted timely, useful, relevant, and incredible insights about how to make informed career choices. His writing is compelling; his stories are captivating; and his lessons learned are priceless. I will readily recommend this book to any aspiring professional who wants to make thoughtful personal career choices. This is the best book I have seen on navigating a career journey."

–Dave Ulrich, Professor at University of Michigan, Ranked #1 management educator and guru

D0951862

"I found myself empathizing and being entertained while reading this enthralling book. I couldn't put it down once I started reading. His personal insights into the Lehman bankruptcy, the tough decisions of whether to change employers, and dealing with difficult issues such as being laid off are engaging and real. The career and life lessons he shares are invaluable."

–W. Steve Albrecht, Board member of Red Hat, Cypress Semiconductor, and SkyWest Airlines

"Nathan knows what it takes to succeed in today's business world. This book is a must-read for anyone striving to launch a successful career."

–David Bradford, Chairman of HireVue, Former CEO of Fusion-IO, Author of *Up Your Game*

"After a volatile and brief career on Wall Street where he went through the Lehman Brothers bankruptcy and other setbacks, Nathan Tanner explored corporate alternatives before returning to graduate school for an MBA and a new career in HR. His book is about the range of his experiences, many under great pressure, and the essential lessons he learned from them. These lessons are invaluable for undergraduates and young professionals, as well as for HR veterans struggling to understand millennial motivations."

–Kim Smith, Managing Director of BYU Peery Institute of Financial Services, Over twenty-five years with Goldman Sachs

Not Your Parents' Workplace

NOT YOUR PARENTS' WORKPLACE

Critical lessons for interns and young professionals

NATHAN TANNER

Author's Note

To respect the privacy of friends and colleagues, names and identifying details of the people portrayed in this book have been changed.

The views and opinions expressed in this book are my own and in no way represent those held by former, current, or future employers.

If any of these organizations are viewed unfavorably after reading this book, I apologize in advance. This was not my intention. It was a privilege to work at each of these companies.

Contents

"Everybody has a plan until
they get punched in the mouth"

–Mike Tyson

Introduction

The business world has changed significantly over the past few decades. We all know that. The days of joining a company, rising steadily through the ranks, and retiring with a comfortable pension are long gone. My dad worked at two companies during the first 30 years of his career. In contrast, within a year of graduation I had already worked at three, enduring the largest bankruptcy in history at one company and getting laid off by another. Like many of you, I planned on one thing, but events and circumstances outside of my control forced me to pivot.

I knew the business world would be different from my father's, but I didn't realize how quickly things would change for my generation. The Millennial generation—individuals born between the early 1980s and early 2000s—are walking into a very different business environment than the one in which our parents worked. We can't rely on the stability of a career path within a single company. To be successful in this new world, we must take a proactive approach to managing our careers.

My goal is not to describe how the workplace has changed (this topic has been covered by countless others). Rather, my goal in writing this book is two-fold. I hope to share an intimate and transparent account of the highs and lows I've experienced as a young professional, but more importantly, I hope to teach insightful lessons that will help you find your dream job and be successful in your career.

I've been fascinated with career management since my days as an undergraduate student. During my final year at Brigham Young University (BYU), I worked as the president of the Investment Banking Club and helped place more than 50 students in Wall Street positions. I later helped my classmates strengthen their professional network while serving as the president of our alumni chapter in San Francisco.

As a graduate student pursuing a Masters of Business Administration (MBA) degree, I worked on the career services team helping students develop networking and interviewing skills. I currently serve as a LinkedIn Ambassador teaching students and young professionals how to effectively use LinkedIn. I've been a guest lecturer in numerous career management courses and have spent countless hours helping people one-on-one. Throughout these experiences I've learned what works and what doesn't.

While this book highlights a lot of my experiences in finance, the lessons shared are applicable to anyone pursuing a business career. These lessons include:

- How to network and build strong professional relationships (Chapters 1, 5, 10)
- How to gain experience beyond internships (Chapter 1)
- How to prepare for interviews, including how to tell your "story" (Chapter 2)
- How to make the most of your internship (Chapters 2, 3)
- Deciding whether to quit your job (Chapter 6)
- Why you shouldn't underestimate culture fit (Chapter 6)
- Why finding the right people to work with is more important than your job function (Chapter 7)
- Whether you should pursue an MBA or other graduate programs (Chapter 9)
- How to develop a professional competitive advantage (Chapter 9)

At the end of the book, there are two appendices. Appendix A is a brief guide teaching how to hold effective informational interviews (a critical part of networking), and Appendix B lists my favorite books that are relevant to students and young professionals.

I believe the stories and lessons shared in this book will help you launch a meaningful career, take charge of your future, and maximize your potential. In short, I believe that sharing how I found my path will help you find yours. Let's get started.

1

Provo to Manhattan

As the plane touched down at JFK International Airport, the same thought kept running through my mind: *What am I doing here?* It was 5:30 AM, and following a cross-country red-eye flight, I had just arrived in New York City. In less than an hour I would be joining a handful of classmates to meet professionals from the top firms on Wall Street. I had spent much of my savings to go on this trip, and although I wasn't completely sure why I made the investment, I needed to make the most of it.

A few months earlier, the world of investment banking had been foreign. I was then a sophomore at BYU in Provo, Utah, and I'd recently been accepted to the undergrad business school. I wanted to find the best job I could land, but I didn't know which opportunities to pursue.

I started applying for business internships, and after many rejections, I got an interview with Fidelity Investments in Salt Lake City. I was ecstatic. I spent a few minutes reading the corporate website, put on my suit and tie, and headed to the office. I clearly hadn't prepared, but at the time I didn't know any better.

I waited anxiously in the lobby until two seasoned investment advisors invited me back to a small conference room. A few questions into the interview they asked, "Can you please tell us about a time when you showed initiative?" My mind went blank. I couldn't think of anything to say. After a few seconds, I thought about the girl in my finance class. She was very attractive, and I enjoyed sitting next to her each class period. I wanted to ask her on a date, but I was nervous. I didn't know how she would respond, and I didn't want things to get awkward if she turned me down. I finally summoned all the courage I could muster and asked her out. She said yes, and we had a great time on our date.

I knew this wasn't the kind of story they were looking for, but I couldn't think of a better response. The silence started getting awkward. *Surely it will be better to say something than to just sit here frozen*, I thought. So, I went ahead and shared the story. When I finished, I knew my hopes of landing the internship were also finished. The interviewers were polite, but I could tell they were wondering, *Who decided to interview this weirdo?* The official news came a few days later, and as expected, I didn't get the job. (I did eventually get the girl, but that's another story.)

Weeks later I attended a BYU event where local professionals discussed their careers in financial services. It was sponsored by the Investment Banking Club, and several of the guest speakers had started their careers in investment banking. Wanting to learn more, I approached a well-dressed student representing the club.

"So, you are with the Investment Banking Club..." I asked, trying to strike up a conversation.

"Yeah, I'm Greg. Have you ever heard of investment banking?" he fired back, not knowing whether to brush me off or take me seriously.

"Well kind of," I lied. "I just got into the business program, and I'll be studying finance."

"Do you know what you want to do in banking?" he inquired. "There's sales and trading, private wealth management, research, M&A." I didn't know how to respond. As the surrounding circle grew, I felt added pressure to say something intelligent, but I just stood there.

"Getting into investment banking is almost impossible," Greg continued. "You need either a perfect GPA or strong connections in the industry. Few BYU students get into investment banking. Most of the kids who make it are from Harvard, Princeton, and other Ivy League schools."

With that, the conversation came to an abrupt halt. I continued to stand there, awkwardly, but Greg turned to the student next to me. This student looked so eager I wanted to stay and hear their conversation. She told Greg that she loved investment banking and knew she wanted to get into M&A.

"In fact," she said, "I've wanted to do investment banking for years. I'll do anything to break into the industry!" I found her enthusiasm slightly obnoxious, but in hindsight I was clearly jealous of her knowledge.

They discussed M&A for a few more minutes, but I had heard enough. I had no clue what they were talking about, and I wasn't about to embarrass myself any further. The event had been a disaster. Not only did I walk away without any insights on how to start my career, but I felt like an idiot.

I arrived home and fired up my laptop. Greg may have dismissed me as a potential club member, but I needed to figure some things out, like what M&A stood for and why they had talked about it so long. I pulled up my web browser and googled "MNA." Nothing relevant came up, so I tried "emenay." Google autocorrected my search to the word "enema," but it didn't take long to realize that wasn't what they had talked about. With my efforts thwarted, I dismissed investment banking as a career path and called it a night.

A few days later I received an email inviting me to another Investment Banking Club event. I had written off banking, but I felt that attending another meeting might answer my questions. Two bankers from Lehman Brothers presented an overview of investment banking via video conference. They discussed how new analysts were able to advise executives on billion-dollar transactions and help companies raise money. I learned that college grads who began their careers in a two-year, skill-building analyst training program were highly-coveted by future employers. But the main thing that stood out was how much money first-year analysts made. I was in shock. I thought, *No wonder getting into banking is so difficult.*

That night I called my older brother. "Did you know that investment bankers make over six figures right out of school?" I asked. Like me, he was unfamiliar with Wall Street careers. I continued, "The lifestyle is brutal, but after a few years you have incredible exit options." He told me that making sacrifices early in a career would help in the long run and he encouraged me to pursue it further.

Over the next few months I spent as much time as I could learning about the industry. I read *Liar's Poker*, *The Vault Guide*, and other banking classics. I spoke with everyone I knew who had investment banking experience, including former interns and full-time professionals. The further I went down the path, the better I felt.

As I learned about investment banking, one myth was dispelled. Contrary to what movies portray, most bankers don't sit on a trading floor and yell, "Buy, buy, buy! Sell, sell, sell!" That's one part of the business—sales and trading—but the investment banking division, where the majority of new analysts start, work in a quiet environment. These bankers focus on large transactions that take several months to complete.

Most importantly, I learned that M&A, the topic that Greg and the other student had discussed, stood for mergers and acquisitions. I frequently heard that M&A was the "sexy" place to work, but I wondered how anything in finance could be described as such.

During this period of discovery, the Investment Banking Club announced a networking trip to New York City. Jim Stratton, a former investment banker turned BYU professor, would be leading the small group of students, and those attending would have unique opportunities to network with Wall Street professionals. Eager to visit New York, I signed up for the trip.

So THERE I WAS, having just arrived in the Big Apple. I exited JFK airport and made my way into Manhattan by subway. I thought about the next few days and wondered what would transpire. As I rode the subway I was overcome with mixed emotions. My body was tired after the red-eye flight, but I was nervous and excited for what was in store. I wanted to make a good impression with the bankers I'd be meeting. I thought back to my initial meeting with the Investment

Banking Club. I had left that meeting feeling like a fool, but things were different now. I had done my homework and learned as much as I could about investment banking, but I was still nervous.

I arrived at my subway exit, left the station, and walked up the stairs. A ray of sunlight flashed in my eyes. Massive buildings filled the skyline and yellow taxis swarmed the streets. I wandered around the financial district for a few minutes, trying to find the meeting place. I saw a street sign that stopped me dead in my tracks—*Wall St.* As I stared at the sign, a burst of energy filled my body. Although I was exhausted after sleeping just a few hours on the plane, adrenaline flowed through me and heightened my senses.

Many have said that there's a singular energy in New York City, and I had often wondered what they meant. But as I looked at the sign and watched a sea of professionals make their way to work, I finally understood. I could feel the energy. It was a feeling of opportunity. At that moment I felt like I could achieve anything I wanted.

Arriving at our group's prearranged meeting spot a little early, I pulled out the crumpled piece of paper listing the firms we'd be visiting. All the big names were on there: Goldman Sachs, Morgan Stanley, Lehman Brothers, J.P. Morgan, Bear Stearns, Deutsche Bank, UBS, and Credit Suisse. My classmates soon arrived, and together we started our adventure. The offices were amazing. Each firm had an immaculate interior, beautiful conference rooms, and gorgeous views of the city. I had never seen anything like it. The discussions were informative and provided insight into what it was like to work on Wall Street. There were two firms that stood out (largely because of their contrasting cultures): Bear Stearns and Goldman Sachs.

Ed Morgan, a managing director in fixed income, was the Bear Stearns representative. After a gourmet lunch, Ed introduced himself and got down to business. He was a no-nonsense guy who didn't mind putting people in their place. His large personality permeated the conference room, and I wondered how one person could possess such self-confidence.

"Let me tell you guys one thing about Wall Street," Ed bellowed. "EVERYBODY is here to make money! If there is one thing you guys remember about this trip, it's that EVERYONE on Wall Street wants to make money!"

His boldness caught me off guard, but I was intrigued. "Several years ago," he continued. "I told my wife that if I didn't make a lot of money, I'd never be satisfied." Ed was unlike any professional I'd met, and I had never heard anyone speak so candidly about money. *I guess New York is different*, I thought.

The environment at Goldman Sachs was far less ostentatious. The bankers were more conservative and didn't carry a chip on their shoulders. Then again, it was Goldman Sachs, the premier firm on Wall Street.

Several professionals took us on a brief tour of a trading floor (the same one Michael Lewis worked on when he wrote *Liar's Poker)*. Bankers were screaming across the room, and while I heard what was being said, their financial jargon meant nothing to me.

Following the tour, we entered a conference room to learn more about the Goldman Sachs culture. Much of the presentation highlighted teamwork—the value that supposedly differentiated Goldman from its competitors. All the other banks had claimed something similar, but Goldman's presentation was impressive, and the bankers were all top-notch. I could see why Goldman was the most sought after firm on Wall Street.

After two busy days of company visits, a few of us had dinner at ESPN Zone in Times Square. Two of my classmates were no longer interested in investment banking. Turned off by the long hours and hectic lifestyle, they turned the conversation to other topics. At the other side of the table, I continued discussing the trip with Lauren Avery, one of my classmates. I had enjoyed getting to know her over the last few days. Unlike our classmates, Lauren and I had been energized by the meetings. We were ready to work harder than ever to find a job. We reviewed what we had learned and talked about our aspirations for the future. "So, if you could choose any job at any bank, what would it be?" I asked her.

"Definitely private wealth management at Goldman Sachs," Lauren responded. "What about you?"

I thought through each of the banks we met with, and Lehman Brothers felt like the best fit. For one, I made an immediate connection with Anna Coleman, the BYU grad who led the presentation. She was down-to-earth and seemed like the perfect mentor. Several analysts had discussed their day-to-day life, and one told us how he'd broken an office lamp while playing Wiffle ball at 2:00 AM the night before. They seemed like an easy going group that struck the right balance between working hard and having fun.

More importantly, Lehman's recent track record was impressive. Since 1994 the firm's stock price had increased more than 25% a year. The word constantly being used to describe Lehman's progress was momentum. Goldman Sachs and Morgan Stanley were larger and offered more prestige, but Lehman was a rising star.

I set my drink down, turned to Lauren, and declared, "Investment banking division at Lehman Brothers." Coming to that realization felt good. It was a moment of clarity.

I CAME BACK FROM New York with new perspective. I had a clear vision of where I wanted to start my career and a better idea of how to get there.

Prior to the trip, I had secured a month-long internship with a team of Merrill Lynch financial advisors. It was an unpaid internship, but I felt it was worth the sacrifice. I needed experience. My responsibilities at Merrill weren't that glamorous, and I spent most of my first week filing papers. I wanted to make the most of this internship and asked one of the advisors if I could join her for client meetings. She was happy to let me sit in, and I learned more from these meetings than any of the assigned projects I had been given.

The Merrill Lynch internship came to an end, and my attention turned to the rest of the summer. I wanted to find an investment banking internship, but my chances were slim. I was between my sophomore and junior years and most banks wanted someone a year ahead of me.

During my search, I discovered that my parents' neighbor had a son-in-law, Nate Barber, who was living with them for the summer. Nate had worked as an analyst at J.P. Morgan, and I wanted to learn everything I could from him.

Throughout our discussion I fired dozens of questions at him, trying to glean all that I could from Nate's experiences. At one point we discussed DCA Capital, a local investment bank where he'd recently interviewed. I expressed interest, and Nate said he would happily forward my resume. I told Nate to let them know I was eager to get investment banking experience, and I was willing to work for free if necessary.

A few weeks later, I got a call from one of the partners at DCA Capital. They extended an invitation to interview and wanted me to come in the next day. I stayed up late that night, preparing as best as I could. I showed up to the interview nervous, but prepared, and I reminded myself that under no circumstances would I share any stories from my dating life. That strategy had already backfired.

The partners asked questions about my previous experiences and provided more details about the firm. They didn't have an intern budget, but told me that if I was actually willing to work for free, it might work out. The next day I got a call from one of the partners. Once again, he said that they couldn't compensate me, but they would love to have me aboard.

Working at DCA Capital turned out to be a rich experience. The bankers I worked with were first class and invited me to their partner meetings. I felt like I was given meaningful assignments and got to work on several transactions. The internship assured me that I was on the right path. It was exactly what I wanted.

As my internship at DCA Capital came to a close, I thought about the progress I had made. My trip to New York confirmed my interest in Wall Street, and the two finance internships strengthened both my resume and self-confidence. My goal was to land a job with a top investment bank. I had a plan of attack, but there was still a lot of work to do.

Lessons

1) Learn how to network

Learning how to network is the first and probably most important lesson discussed in this book. Investment banks didn't recruit at BYU, and I was told that if I wanted to get into banking, I had to network my way in. I didn't understand what that meant, but thankfully, I had several classmates willing to help.

Networking isn't about swapping business cards or adding people you've never met to connect on LinkedIn. The key purpose of networking is to *build meaningful, mutually beneficial relationships.* Reaching out to professionals you don't know can be very intimidating and requires an investment of time and effort. Networking is a skill, and like other skills, it can be improved through consistent practice.

Some college students can find a job without learning how to network. Companies anxiously come to campus looking to hire, allowing these students to focus entirely on getting good grades. This isn't a bad strategy, but most of us aren't so fortunate. Even those who land their first job with minimal effort eventually discover that learning to network is critical when finding a new job or seeking a promotion.

During my internship search, a friend recommended that I read Keith Ferrazzi's *Never Eat Alone.* It is the most practical book I've read on developing professional relationships and should be required reading for anyone launching a career in business. (See Appendix B for my favorite takeaways from *Never Eat Alone*.)

2) Get experience

As an undergrad I was turned down for several internships because I didn't have enough experience. This is one of the frustrating realities of the business world. Paid internships are ideal, but there are other ways to get experience if that isn't an option.

After my initial trip to New York, I desperately wanted to work on Wall Street. In order to have a shot, I needed relevant experience on my resume. While I wasn't compensated during my internship with DCA Capital, that experience proved to be essential when I was interviewing with larger banks. With real investment banking experience, I could articulate my passion for the industry and explain why I was a good fit. Several of my peers had better grades and standardized test scores, but my experience made the difference.

For those not in the position to spend a summer working for free, consider experiential courses or part-time internships during the school year. Both will enhance your resume and show potential employers that you're committed.

3) Get comfortable with being uncomfortable

Embarking on a new career path will likely put you in situations where you feel overwhelmed and uncomfortable. Embrace these opportunities! The story of googling "emenay" instead of "M&A" is a favorite. It's ridiculous that I almost wrote off a career path because I was intimidated and didn't understand the jargon. If you can't find an answer to a question, be bold and ask for help.

Whenever you try something new, there's always a level of discomfort. When you avoid uncomfortable situations, you avoid opportunities for personal growth. Don't let fear of the unknown, new lingo, or lack of knowledge prevent you from pursuing a career opportunity. Push forward and embrace the learning process.

4) Make the most of your internship

Interns are often disappointed when their assigned tasks aren't as exciting as they hoped. If you find yourself in this situation, be proactive and find ways to maximize your experience. If there's a specific project you want to get involved with or a skill you want to learn, consider discussing this with your manager. If I had just focused on my assigned tasks at Merrill Lynch, my experience would have been far less rewarding. Be curious, ask a lot of questions, and look for ways to make an impact. It's your responsibility to make it a great internship.

2

Recruiting Season

Before the summer ended, I made trips to New York City and San Francisco to meet with investment banking professionals. If banks weren't going to come to campus, I needed to go to them.

During each trip I set up informational interviews to learn about each bank. As I asked questions and got to know each professional, I better understood the role of investment banking analysts and the cultural nuances of each firm. This was not a one-sided activity. The bankers were taking mental notes on me and trying to decide whether I was a good fit for their firm. (See Appendix A for a guide on informational interviews.)

During these meetings, my goal wasn't just to learn about the firms. I was trying to develop rapport with each professional. In several months I would apply for internships, and I needed them to have enough confidence in me to move my resume to the interview pile.

As I met more bankers, I understood that GPA and standardized test scores would heavily factor into recruiting decisions. This was a big concern. My GPA was half-decent, but my ACT score was atrocious. There was nothing I could do to fix that, so I tried to focus on things I could control—gaining relevant work experience and strengthening my relationships. I needed to find advocates. I felt confident that if I had at least one solid relationship at each bank I'd have a decent shot at getting an interview.

Additionally, I had a very challenging course load that semester. I signed up for an on-campus internship and was enrolled in the Finance Core, which consisted of four difficult finance courses taken together in one semester. There were 40 students in my section, and we stayed in the same room for all four courses. I got to know each student fairly well and built great friendships.

From the first day of class, one student, Mike Robertson, stood out. Mike was mature, confident, and intelligent. He actively participated in discussions and made relevant and insightful comments. To my great fortune, Mike and I ended up on the same team and spent a lot of time together. Like me, Mike was very interested in investment banking. He was just starting the networking process, but Mike had such a strong grasp of finance that he'd likely have no problem finding an internship.

In class one day, Jim Stratton announced that Lehman Brothers was offering a winter internship and hoped to hire a few BYU students. I was surprised by the new opportunity and phoned Anna, my key contact at Lehman, to discuss the internship. I learned that the winter internship would be nearly identical to the summer analyst program that was standard in the industry. Those who performed well during the internship would be offered a full-time position. Anna expressed confidence that I'd be a strong candidate and encouraged me to apply, which I did.

A few days after the application deadline, I got a call from Lehman Brothers. They wanted to interview me. I was thrilled! For the past eight months I'd been working toward an internship like this one and my efforts were starting to pay off. I called a few classmates who interned at Lehman the prior summer. They offered several insights and provided additional resources to help me prepare. The morning of my interview finally came. After hours of study and practice, I felt ready. I was asked the following questions:

1) Tell me how you became interested in investment banking.

2) Why do you want to work for Lehman Brothers?

3) Tell me about a time you worked with a difficult team.

4) Tell me about a time you showed leadership.

5) Tell me about a time you received constructive criticism. How did you handle it?

6) If you have $10,000 of credit card debt and $10,000 invested in an S&P 500 mutual fund, what would you do given the current market situation?

7) If you started a business, what would it be, and how would you maximize profits?

8) Tell me about a time you had to sell something. What was your approach?

9) Pitch me a stock.

10) What questions do you have for me?

Aside from questions seven and eight, the interview was similar to what I expected. A few days later I got a call back from Human Resources (HR). I had passed the first round and would be moving on to a final round in New York.

I had less than a week to prepare, and felt overwhelmed. This was my shot, and I didn't want to blow it. The timing of the interview couldn't have been worse. There were only three weeks left in the semester, and I had fallen behind in several of my courses. I knew I couldn't catch up *and* prepare well for the interview, so I skipped class the last two days before the interview. I was never one to miss class, but I figured I could live with a lower GPA if I landed this internship. It was a risk I was willing to take. In hindsight, it was an obvious choice, but at the time, I felt guilty about missing school.

During my interview preparation, I ran into a friend who had accepted a full-time offer with Goldman Sachs. I told him I was really nervous about technical questions and that most of my time had been spent preparing for them. He pointed out that being ready for such questions was important, but not nearly as important as developing a good story for why I wanted to work in investment banking. Others had mentioned the need to have a compelling story, but until this discussion I hadn't spent much time thinking about mine. This conversation helped me get back on track.

A few BYU classmates joined me for the final round of interviews at Lehman. Mike, my Finance Core teammate, was one of them. Our flight arrived late in the evening, and since all the hotels in Manhattan were full, we stayed in a modest hotel near JFK airport. At breakfast Mike and I didn't say or eat much. We were so anxious about the day's events. Our cab arrived, and although we gave ourselves plenty of time to get to Lehman's midtown headquarters, we immediately hit traffic. This certainly didn't calm our nerves.

After a final review of my prep materials, I closed my notebook and tried to relax. Mike, who would likely be the most prepared candidate, was still very concerned. He was furiously flipping through his notebook, trying to extract every last bit of information. "Hey Nate, do you remember details on the pecking order theory?" Mike anxiously questioned.

"Not really," I responded. Weeks before we had covered this theory in a finance class, but I was drawing a blank.

"Do you think there's a good chance we'll get asked about it today?" he inquired.

"Mike, I think we have a better chance of getting asked about New York sports than the pecking order theory." To calm our nerves, we took turns sharing everything we knew about recent happenings with the Yankees, Mets, Giants, and Knicks.

The light mood came to a halt when the already bad traffic grew worse. We were 10 blocks shy of our destination but the cab wasn't moving. The clock read 11:55 AM, which left us only five minutes to reach the Lehman headquarters. We quickly paid the driver, grabbed our bags and started running through Times Square. We arrived at the office a few minutes late and a bit sweaty, but things were fine.

I had four one-on-one interviews that were 30 minutes each. I was asked more behavioral questions than technical ones, and I sensed that the interviewers were gauging my "fit" with the firm's culture. Several questions centered on my internship with DCA Capital. The interviewers wanted to know what I had learned and were impressed by my willingness to take an unpaid internship.

I was surprised to see Anna, the lead BYU contact, as one of the interviewers. I was also surprised that her interview was more challenging than the rest. Rather than ask typical banking questions about valuing companies, her questions centered on valuing a home under various financing scenarios. I was unprepared for these questions, and I stumbled a bit as I walked through each scenario. As the interview was winding down, Anna pulled out a copy of my transcript and identified a course I had taken—Descriptive Astronomy. She raised her eyebrows and inquired, "D+... What happened there?"

I frantically thought of an explanation, but simply responded, "Umm, it was freshman year." She nodded and grinned.

I was ecstatic to find out a few days later that I got an internship offer. I called Mike and discovered that he had also received an offer. We both accepted and made plans to start together in January. I had landed my dream internship with a top investment bank, but the journey was far from over.

Lessons

1) Prepare for interviews

Prepping for interviews may seem obvious, but I'm surprised by the number of students and young professionals who neglect such an important task. Many are willing to stay up late to study for an exam or work on a project, but they only take a few minutes to prep for an interview. I remember a roommate of mine who came home from school one day in disappointment. He'd just been rejected by his top company. When I asked what he'd done to prepare for the interview, he looked confused. My roommate was intelligent and got good grades, but he probably should have spent more time improving his interviewing skills.

I believe the best way to start preparing for an interview is to connect with current employees. They can tell you what to expect and provide an insider's view into the recruiting process. Reviewing the company on Glassdoor can also be valuable. There you can read about people's interview experiences and learn a lot about a company's culture. Finding a list of commonly asked questions for your job function is also helpful. While this won't prepare you for all questions, it will cover many of the basic ones. Finally, take time to do a mock interview. Ask a friend or roommate for help. If that isn't an option, practice in the mirror.

2) Craft a compelling story

As I mentioned earlier, it's important to have a good story. What does that even mean? The interviewer wants to know more about your experiences and why you're a good fit for the job. Frequently, interviewers will invite you to walk through your resume or tell them about yourself. While it may be tempting to discuss every bullet on your resume, resist the urge. This is your chance to share the highlights of your work experience, and, most importantly, share why you are the best person for the job. You may look at your resume and see a collection of unrelated positions, but in every resume there's a great story waiting to be told.

3) Don't forget to ask questions

At the end of almost every interview, the interviewee is given the chance to ask questions. Don't turn down this opportunity! Asking intelligent questions can be a great way to set yourself apart and express your interest in the company and position.

It's wise to cater your questions to each interviewer. If you get an interview agenda in advance, review the LinkedIn profiles of your interviewers to get a sense of their roles and backgrounds. When they introduce themselves, pay attention to what they say and ask questions that are relevant to their background.

Always make sure that your questions are appropriate for that person's level. For instance, avoid asking junior employees about details of the company's long-term strategy. They probably won't know the answer and may feel embarrassed. Finally, avoid questions that can be easily answered by looking at the company's website. Ask questions that show you've done your homework.

4) Start your search early

Following my Lehman internship, I served as the president of the BYU Investment Banking Club. My goal was to introduce students to Wall Street careers and help them prepare for such jobs. I regularly met one-on-one with students interested in banking. I found a high correlation between students who started their job search early and those who landed at a top bank. Not surprisingly, those who started late rarely accomplished their goals.

When you start networking with professionals *before you need a job*, they are far more likely to help. Several professionals have told me that many people only reach out when they want a job. At that point, it's often too late in the process. Start your search early.

3

The Internship

Mike and I exited the subway at 50th Street and started the short walk to Lehman's headquarters. It was the first day of our internship, and we were filled with anticipation. We turned the corner and immediately recognized the colossal building we would call home for the next ten weeks.

Mike walked through the main door, but my mind was elsewhere, and I didn't give him enough space. It was a revolving door, and we ended up entering at the same time. The doors came to an immediate halt. We were stuck. Eventually we discovered that taking tiny, synchronized steps was the only way to get the door moving. Each step inched the door open a little further, and after what seemed like an eternity, we reached the other side. We were in.

By this point, a long line of frustrated investment bankers was outside the building. These bankers were impatiently waiting to walk inside and start their busy day. I felt like such a moron and prayed that none of them would be in my new group. *What a way to start my big internship*, I thought.

The first few days were spent in training. We learned more about the firm's culture and strengthened our Microsoft Excel skills. But the highlight came on day three when they issued us BlackBerry phones—the ultimate status symbol of a banker, or so I thought. I had heard that BlackBerrys served as electronic leashes meant to keep bankers tied to work at all times, but I didn't care. I kept mine attached to my belt holster, like a cowboy would wear his six shooter. I thought I was so cool.

During the daytime Mike and I focused on training, but we spent most of our evenings hunting down mattresses. I had been responsible for finding housing, and although our new place was mostly furnished, there were no mattresses to be found. Leveraging Craigslist, Mike found a mattress 15 blocks south of our apartment. We didn't want to rent a truck, so we carried the mattress above our heads as we walked down Broadway—one of the busiest streets in Manhattan—back to our apartment. The looks we got from shopkeepers and random people walking down the street were priceless.

I didn't feel comfortable buying a used mattress online, but after several nights of sleeping on the wood floor I needed to find something. Trips to nearby mattress stores were fruitless since I couldn't afford anything at such high prices. There was a mattress discounter on the other side of town, so Mike and I headed there after training one night. After scouring the store I found a twin mattress that would work. It was only a few inches thick and hardly ideal, but the price couldn't be beat. Now I just had to find a way to get it home. We were too far to carry it back to our apartment, and we weren't allowed to bring it on the subway. I thought, *Maybe we could fit it in the back seat of a cab*. There was only one way to find out.

Mike flagged down a taxi, and when the driver saw us he immediately waved his hands and yelled, "No! No! No! You can't bring that in here!" But it was too late. I had already opened the rear door and began stuffing it in. I jumped in the back seat while Mike finished shoving the mattress into the taxi. After a few attempts at slamming the door, it finally closed. Somehow we had made it work.

As we headed back to the apartment, our driver started screaming expletives out the window. I couldn't see what was going on because the mattress was completely wrapped around me, blocking all of the windows. We came to a stop light, and I heard a man in another car cursing at our driver. Not being able to see anything, I yelled, "Mike, what's going on out there!?" Apparently our driver had cut off the cab next to him, and the other driver retaliated by throwing an open water bottle. *Welcome to New York*, I thought.

After what seemed like an eternity, our taxi accelerated, and we continued the journey home. We arrived at our apartment and Mike helped me carry the mattress upstairs. My new mattress, however pathetic it may have been, allowed me to finally get a decent night's rest. And I would need every moment of sleep I could get over the next few months.

Training came to an end and I was introduced to my team, the Consumer/Retail group. I quickly observed that my team didn't fit the negative investment banking stereotypes portrayed in Hollywood movies. The group was very diverse, and they all seemed to treat each other with respect. There wasn't a single Gordon Gekko-type banker on the team.

My favorite person at Lehman worked a few floors below me. I nicknamed him Daddy Warbucks. He was an obese, sharply-dressed man with black, slicked-back hair. He wore black suspenders emblazoned with gold dollar signs and walked with such swagger you'd have thought he was the CEO. I never got to meet him, but I'll always remember Daddy Warbucks as a living caricature of Wall Street culture.

After introducing myself to the team, I found my desk in a jungle of cubicles. I sat next to two analysts, Alex and Luke. Like me, Alex had gone to a university not heavily recruited by investment banks. Unlike me, he had a pet Chihuahua named Google. When Brittany Spears went crazy and shaved her head, Alex assembled a 3-D paper cutout of her head and attached it to the top of his monitor. He may have had some quirks, but Alex was a great guy. He was happier than most of the analysts and went out of his way to welcome me to the team.

My favorite story about Alex occurred during a phone call he had with one of the associates, who are usually MBA grads and are one level above analysts. The associate was giving Alex instructions on a pitch book, and though he politely agreed with what the associate was saying, Alex was irritated. When the call ended he slammed the phone down and pounded his desk. "This ruins everything!" Alex yelled. "Now I can't go to the tanning salon tonight!"

Luke, the other analyst I sat by, had gone to Wharton, the top undergrad business program in the nation. Located in Philadelphia, Wharton was an investment banking factory that sent swarms of graduates to Wall Street each year. Summer internship recruiting was underway, and I often heard Luke tell Wharton candidates that Lehman Brothers was the only decent bank on Wall Street. All the others were, in his opinion, garbage.

One intern candidate made the mistake of revealing that she was considering a Merrill Lynch offer. Appalled, Luke told her that that choosing Merrill over Lehman was like going to a community college when you could go to Wharton. I was astonished by his arrogance and wondered who should be more offended, Merrill Lynch or the countless students enrolled at community colleges.

The investment banking lifestyle was just as strenuous as expected. I typically arrived at the office by 9:00 AM and didn't leave until after midnight. 80-hour weeks were the standard. Thankfully there were a few perks that made the daily grind more bearable. Each night we were allotted $25 to order dinner from Seamless, an online service of 100+ restaurants that delivered right to our office. If I stayed past 9:00 PM, which I did most nights, I was driven home in a black car.

These perks softened the burden of working long hours, but I was amazed at how frequently I heard analysts complain about them. If someone's black car arrived a few minutes late, we'd all hear about it the next day. One night an analyst received the wrong dinner order. He pulled the food from his bag and threw it in the trash, horrified. "This is NOT what I ordered!"

I got irritated when colleagues complained about minuscule problems, but I occasionally caught myself acting the same way. I learned that when operating on only a few hours of sleep it's easy to find fault in almost everything.

A few weeks into the internship one of the managing directors pulled me aside. He needed me to update the league tables—a chart that ranked each bank on a set of criteria such as revenue or total transactions completed. We had an important pitch in a few days, and he wanted to prove we were the firm of choice. League tables often factored into clients' decisions, and we needed to show that we had done more relevant deals than anyone else. I sliced the data several different ways, but I still couldn't get our firm ranked number one.

I approached the managing director, handed him the data, and summarized my efforts. He looked at the league tables for a moment, tossed them back to me, and blurted, "This is banking, not boy scouts. Find a way to get us to the top."

With that, our conversation ended and he walked away. Alex showed me some tricks, and I eventually managed to get Lehman ranked number one. I guess you could say that the first internship lesson I learned was how to manipulate data to make our firm look good. We didn't lie, but I wondered what the client would think when every investment bank they were considering claimed to be the top-ranked advisor.

As an intern, most of my work centered on helping other analysts on transactions. I spent a lot of time preparing comparable company analyses, or *comps* as they are commonly referred to in the industry. For example, if I were trying to find a valuation for Kraft

Foods, I would make a list of companies similar to Kraft and find valuation ratios (enterprise value to revenue, price to earnings, etc.) for each. I would then take those ratios and multiply them by Kraft's revenue or net income to get an implied valuation. The calculations were straight forward, but finding all of the data required hours of digging through financial statements and legal documents.

Other methods of valuing a company included precedent transactions analysis (analyzing similar companies that were recently acquired) and discounted cash flow analysis (forecasting future cash flows and using an interest rate to discount the cash flows to today's value). The companies we advised were involved in billion-dollar transactions, and investment bankers made money by charging a fee, typically about 1% of the total transaction value.

One day I arrived at the office to find out I had been staffed on an important pitch our group head would be making the next day. I spent the day working on the presentation materials. Around 5:00 PM, Natasha, the associate, came by to check on my progress. Natasha asked when the slides would be complete, and I thought I told her a *portion* would be done in 15 minutes. I must have said that *everything* would be completed in 15 minutes, because a half hour later she stopped by again, wondering why it wasn't ready. I explained that there had been a mix up, and tensions increased as we realized just how much work needed to be done. Natasha didn't yell, but I could sense her frustration and disappointment. I felt awful about the situation and wondered whether I had just blown my chance of getting a full-time offer.

I spent the rest of the night finishing the presentation, and at 3:30 AM, I printed the books and delivered them to our group head. I was physically and emotionally drained. I had literally worked 17 hours straight. The ride home was peaceful, and I looked forward to a few hours of sleep.

Upon arriving at home, I thanked my driver and used all my energy to exit the car. I was so exhausted. I walked to the door and reached into my pocket, but felt nothing. *Where are my keys?* I thought. I tried the other pockets before searching my bag. Still no keys. My heart sank to my stomach as I realized what happened. The keys had fallen out of my pocket during the ride home and I had no way of getting in touch with the driver.

I was locked out of the building and our apartment was on the fifth floor. I banged on the door, hoping a kind soul might wake up and let me in, but no one came. I looked down at my watch. It was almost 4:00 AM.

I tried calling Mike, but it went right to voicemail. I then dialed my other roommate, William. I felt guilty calling so late, but he was my last hope. The phone rang, but no one answered. It was mid-February and far too cold to stay outside the rest of the night. I needed to find shelter for a couple hours.

I looked around and saw an open diner just a block down the road. I started my way to the diner, hoping the manager would let me rest inside. A few steps into my walk I felt my phone vibrating. It was William. He had woken up and was on his way downstairs. I can't describe the joy I felt.

The next morning I spoke with Natasha and apologized for the miscommunication. She told me not to worry and was happy that I delivered the books on time without errors. I was impressed with how Natasha handled the situation. Many bankers would have gone off on me for messing up, but she was very understanding.

This project taught me the importance of communicating clearly, and throughout the rest of my internship, I made an effort to provide frequent updates on my projects. I sometimes thought I was over-communicating, but my coworkers seemed to appreciate it.

The last day of my internship came, and I anxiously awaited my final performance review. The recruiter shared feedback she had gathered from my team. We discussed what I had done well and where I could improve. I don't remember much of our discussion, but the words I was hoping to hear finally came: "We're excited to offer you a full-time position at Lehman Brothers."

I was elated and told her that I planned on accepting the offer. I took this opportunity to express interest in other offices, something I had thought about but hadn't discussed. I was interested in the Silicon Valley office, and I had contacted several analysts to learn more about it.

In the long-term I preferred to live in California, where I grew up, and I wondered if it made sense to start full-time on the West Coast. Many argued that it was wise to launch a finance career in New York. Their argument was that most of the deals were completed by our New York bankers and working at Lehman's headquarters would provide a richer experience. I listened to everyone's advice, but it never felt right to me. Maybe it was the sardine-packed subway rides to work, or the hassle of doing laundry and grocery shopping in a big city. New York had been fun, but it felt consuming at times.

The recruiting team kindly arranged for me to visit Lehman's Silicon Valley office. Located in the suburbs of Menlo Park, the office had a large team of bankers that advised technology companies. I had been warned about working in a regional office—away from the deal flow—but the majority of tech companies were based in Silicon Valley, so I felt confident I'd have a great experience. After thinking about the decision, I accepted the offer to join the Silicon Valley office. Some questioned my reasoning, but the Bay Area just felt like a better fit. I was confident I had made the right decision and was eager to start working.

Lessons

Towards the end of the internship I made a list of lessons I learned during my 10 weeks at Lehman. Regardless of your industry, I believe these are valuable lessons for interns and new hires.

1) **Always know the details of your internship project.** Almost every time you cross paths with others, you'll be asked about your project. If you can clearly articulate what you are working on and have a good attitude, most people will assume you are intelligent and hard working.

2) **After someone gives you an assignment, restate what you need to do in your own words.** If you just smile and nod, it will be assumed you clearly understand the assignment. Avoid getting back to your desk and wasting time trying to figure out what they said. Taking good notes can help.

3) **Being smart and good with numbers is important, but not all that it takes to succeed.** Being resourceful will take you far, and you can save a lot of time by leveraging the work of your peers. If you don't know how to do something, find someone who can teach you. Don't underestimate the importance of communication.

4) **Always be able to reference how you got to a certain output (Excel calculations, research reports, etc).** Your manager will likely ask how you got to a certain number, and you'll look smart if you have the data readily available.

5) **Exercise.** There are few concerns that a good workout can't wash away. If you work in an office where staying late is the expectation, taking time to exercise can be a nice break in the day. Don't neglect your physical and emotional well-being.

6) **When you meet a new person and don't know their title, always guess a level above what you think.** There's no harm in guessing a higher title. It might even make their day.

If I could go back and add one more lesson it would be this—do whatever it takes to get a full-time offer. Even if the company isn't a good fit and you have no desire to return, receiving a full-time offer will give you more options and validate your competency to future employers.

As I stated earlier, I'm a huge proponent of internships. As an intern, no one expects you to be the expert. Ask questions and be curious. You only have a short time to make a lasting impression, but an internship is a great opportunity to gain hands-on experience, develop deep relationships, and advance your career.

4

The Largest Bankruptcy in History

"I want you all to know that Lehman Brothers has been through worse. We'll bounce back stronger than ever. Don't listen to the naysayers. This firm has been around since 1850 and we'll be just fine."

With that, the well-tailored man sporting a thick beard and even thicker New York accent finished his lecture and left the room. I looked around wondering how many of my peers believed him. It was the first week of analyst training, and I was one of 150 newly-hired analysts in the training room.

Much had changed since I completed my internship a year before. Just a few months before training, Bear Stearns was on the brink of bankruptcy and needed a last minute acquisition by J.P. Morgan to save the firm. Many argued Lehman Brothers was next, but none of the Lehman veterans sounded worried. Despite their confidence, the concern among the newly-hired analysts was palpable.

Lehman was in trouble because it had placed big bets on mortgage-related securities. The firm financed these investments by taking on massive amounts of debt. At its peak, Lehman had a debt-to-equity ratio in the neighborhood of 60 to 1, which meant that over 98% of the firm's assets were debt financed. This wasn't a problem in good times, but when the markets turned south, Lehman got into trouble.

The stock had reached an all-time high during my internship, peaking at over $80 per share. But by the time training started, the price had fallen to $22, and we were all keeping a close eye on it. Our internet activity was closely monitored, and at one point it was shut off. Apparently too many of us had been distracted by watching the falling stock.

By the end of our six-week training, Lehman's share price had fallen to $12, down 85% since my intern days. I was concerned, but I didn't realize how grievous the situation was becoming. I still had the vigor of a new hire and was excited for the future.

With analyst training under my belt, I flew across the country to start at the Silicon Valley office. A few days in, I got a call from the associate responsible for staffing analysts. She assigned me to prepare materials for an urgent meeting scheduled at the end of the week. I immediately got started and worked 72 of the next 80 hours, averaging less than 2 hours of sleep each night. I was completely exhausted by the end of it, but I felt proud that I had worked on something meaningful. Nothing ever came of the meeting, and though Lehman was still in trouble, we wouldn't have guessed it by the workload being carried.

I worked on several assignments over the next few weeks, but they came to a halt in early September. The financial markets had worsened and more investment analysts predicted it was only a matter of time until Lehman Brothers would be forced to close its doors. I kept a detailed journal of the events and tried to capture what my colleagues and I experienced during Lehman's final week. I've provided a summarized version of my account.

Tuesday, September 9

Our stock fell 45% today. Over the last week there have been talks that KDB, a Korean bank, was planning to invest roughly $5 billion into the firm. Today those talks came to an end. Everyone in the office was trying to make sense of the day's events. Many feel that if we don't receive a major investment, Lehman is doomed.

It's 2:00 AM, and I'm just wrapping things up at the office. I've been working on a big M&A pitch book for a meeting next week. A lot of the work is formatting and moving logos around, nothing too exciting, but it still needs to look perfect.

I took a break around 9:00 PM and went to a Palo Alto bar with Jonathan and Vanya, two analysts from my group. I don't drink, but I didn't want to miss out on what my colleagues were saying. Vanya, a second-year analyst, shared a few insights about the office culture and told us what we needed to do to get a top-tier performance rating. She expressed concerns about her job and speculated what might happen in the coming days.

Wednesday, September 10

In an effort to dispel market rumors and calm investors, Lehman pre-announced earnings this morning, a week earlier than expected. The quarterly results were close to what analysts predicted—a $3.9 billion loss (Lehman's largest loss since going public) and $7.8 billion in asset write-downs. The firm also announced four "strategic initiatives" to weather the financial storm. They included:

- Selling 55% of Neuberger Berman, the firm's investment management group.

- Cutting the dividend to $0.05.

- Spinning off a vast majority of the firm's commercial real estate assets into a new, separate publicly-traded company.

- Reducing holdings in residential mortgages, commercial real estate and other less liquid assets.

Following the earnings announcement, Frank Stanford, the head of our office, called a meeting to discuss the situation. He encouraged everyone to be calm. "I've been at the firm 31 years, and I've seen worse," Frank declared. He promised that Lehman would pull through and everything would work out for the best.

As I walked out of the conference room I overheard a few associates and vice presidents. "He always gives this speech," one said. "I'm not buying it anymore."

Thursday, September 11

I just got to the office and it's chaotic. I knew it would be a tough day when I saw Lehman's stock price fall to $4, down another 45%. I guess investors didn't find our "strategic initiatives" very convincing.

Fear and panic have taken over. No one was doing any kind of work. Several analysts stopped by and asked, "So what do you think of all this?" I didn't have a response. I don't know what to think, and I wasn't alone. Everyone is afraid that they will soon be out of a job, but it's the senior bankers who are most worried.

On my way to the restroom I bumped into Frank, the head of our office. He looked awful, like someone had punched him in the stomach. I asked how he was holding up, and he was candid: "The market is throwing up all over us today. This is the worst I have ever seen things. We're in real trouble." I wondered what happened to the man who just 24 hours earlier had been confident and optimistic.

Throughout the day a steady stream of rumors were passed around, each one predicting a different fate. Several firms have been mentioned as potential buyers for Lehman, but it all seems to be speculation. Goldman Sachs was the most recent suitor, but that idea was squashed when a Goldman executive denied the rumor.

In the afternoon we had a brief meeting to review the M&A pitch book. The managing director looked over the materials and said they were fine for now. She believes the meeting will likely be cancelled and doesn't want us wasting our time.

Friday, September 12

Lehman's stock dropped another 13% today. With each passing day the firm's future looks increasingly bleak. The latest rumor was that if Lehman doesn't find a buyer this weekend, the firm would be forced to declare bankruptcy. But no one seemed to know whether the rumor was true. To lighten the atmosphere, a few senior bankers ordered pizza for the office. The mood was surprisingly jovial as we gathered and ate in our main conference room.

Shortly after lunch the Federal Reserve announced that they had no plans to provide aid should a foreign bank acquire Lehman. There had been rumors of an acquisition by Barclays, but the firm was only interested if the Federal Reserve guaranteed Lehman's toxic assets. Lehman executives announced that they are confident they can complete a deal over the weekend.

Saturday, September 13

I experienced a wide range of emotions today. I kept telling myself that if Lehman goes under and I'm out of a job, the world isn't over. But I can't shake the feeling that something bad is about to happen. I'm worried, and honestly, a little frustrated. I've worked hard and made sacrifices to get to this point. When I accepted my full-time offer, everything seemed perfect. I planned to work as a Lehman analyst for two years then spend the next two to three years in private equity or at a tech company. After that, I'd likely get an MBA. Now, only a few months into my plan, all bets are off.

I spent a good part of the afternoon speaking with friends and contacts in finance. Several told me to begin looking for a job and to keep looking until I find one or Lehman's troubles get sorted out. I've been told that the skills learned in investment banking are highly sought after by other companies. This may be my chance to give that a test. A second-year analyst shared a list of recruiters and encouraged me to connect with them. I spent the day reaching out to them and working on my resume.

Midway through the afternoon I learned that the Federal Reserve, the SEC, and top executives from each of the major Wall Street firms are meeting in New York to discuss a possible outcome for Lehman Brothers. If a solution is not reached by Sunday evening—when the Asian markets open—it's predicted that Lehman will declare bankruptcy. I'm hopeful, but the government entities continue to stress they won't provide funding to facilitate a deal. Lehman is on its own. There will be no bailout.

Sunday, September 14

While I didn't have any work to complete, I stopped by the office to see who was around. I heard that Barclays backed out of a potential deal but reports said that Bank of America is still in the mix. I was surprised to see most of the analysts and a few associates in the office. Several of them were printing confidential documents and sending proprietary models to their personal email accounts. Warning messages from compliance were ignored.

Many of my colleagues are frustrated we haven't heard from our CEO, Dick Fuld. For years he's been one of the most visible CEOs on Wall Street, but he's been very quiet over the past week.

During dinner I learned that talks with Bank of America came to an end. A conference call with our office declared the inevitable—there will be no deal and the firm will be forced to declare bankruptcy. At 9:00 PM I received the following email:

"This evening, Lehman Brothers Holdings Inc. announced it intends to file a petition under Chapter 11 of the U.S. Bankruptcy Code with the United States Bankruptcy Court for the Southern District of New York. We will be open for business on Monday, September 15 and we will have more information to communicate at that time."

Monday, September 15

At 8:15 AM our office huddled inside the main conference room one last time. A sad and depressing feeling hung in the air. Frank told everyone that it was a pleasure to work together and wished us the best in our future endeavors.

With nothing to do, I went home to polish my resume and make a few calls. I called a friend to see if his firm was hiring, but he kindly shared that I'd have little chance of getting hired—I didn't have enough experience. Other calls yielded similar responses. I had been excited to look for a new job, but I'm realizing it will be harder than anticipated. For several weeks I've been pulled back and forth. I've been hoping for the best, but reality is starting to sink in. *Lehman is bankrupt*, I thought. *And soon I'll be out of a job.*

My thoughts turned to the horrific job market and I wondered whether I should look for work outside of banking. I've had a poor experience so far and the negative culture has taken a toll. Then again, these are unprecedented times. Surely I would have had a better experience if my firm hadn't imploded.

Tuesday, September 16

At 7:30 AM I rolled out of bed and checked my BlackBerry. A deal had been struck! Barclays agreed to acquire the U.S. operations of Lehman Brothers. I headed into the office and found a refreshing buzz in the air. There was a stark contrast between the energy and excitement in the office today and the gloom of yesterday's farewell meeting. We gathered in a conference room—the same one where we held so many emotional meetings over the past week. Everyone was pumped. Smiles filled the room.

Frank quieted us down and delivered a speech for the ages. He discussed the setbacks we experienced over the last few months and promised that the Barclays acquisition would make us stronger than ever. He wrapped it up by bellowing, "I want everyone to get on the phone with their clients. Tell them that we're back in business!"

Lessons

1) Everyone is vulnerable.

When I arrived at Lehman, I admirably looked up to our managing directors, the most senior investment bankers. They led huge deals, had corner offices, and took home big pay checks. By all accounts, they had made it. They carried themselves with confidence and, as *The Bonfire of the Vanities* described them, they were the masters of the universe.

As Lehman fell apart, I realized that it was all a façade. These so-called "masters" were exposed to more risk than most had estimated. Many senior bankers received massive sums of Lehman Brothers stock which the bankruptcy rendered completely worthless. Of the many things I remember from the week leading up to Lehman's bankruptcy, the most vivid memory is the fear I saw in Frank Stanford. I thought he was invincible, but I learned that he was just as vulnerable as the rest of us.

2) Focus on what you can control

During the months leading to Lehman's bankruptcy, I wasted a lot of time worrying about the future. *What if Lehman goes under? What happens if I lose my job?* These worries frequently consumed my thoughts, but I rarely took any action.

I've learned that worrying only makes sense if it

drives you to change behavior. If you're not going to take action, constantly fretting about the future only bogs you down. With that said, focusing on things you can control, and ignoring the things you can't, is far more difficult in practice.

3) Don't chase others

Much has been said of Dick Fuld, Lehman's CEO. During the 2000s, Fuld was insistent on growing Lehman into an investment banking powerhouse. Goldman Sachs and Morgan Stanley were the most dominant, and according to many, Fuld was obsessed with trying to surpass them. Since Lehman didn't have the asset base of Goldman or Morgan, it achieved outsized revenue growth by pursuing increasingly riskier strategies. The firm made massive bets on asset-backed securities, and when the market turned south, the firm imploded.

As I watched Lehman go under and pondered the future of my career, I asked myself several questions. *Was I any different from Fuld? Why did I pursue this path in the first place? Did I go into banking because it was the right fit for me, or did prestige, compensation, and future career options drive my decision?* Lehman got into trouble by focusing on others when it should have focused on what was best for the firm. Consider asking yourself whether your reasons for choosing a career path are the right ones.

5

The Worst Four Months of my Life

January 14, 2009. I remember it like it was yesterday. Frank, our group head, tapped me on the shoulder and asked, "Can you please swing by my office?" At that moment I knew it was over. I sheepishly followed him, like a school boy being escorted to the principal's office. My heart pounded uncontrollably.

Our conversation lasted only a minute or two. He thanked me for my work and told me that times were tough. Cuts needed to be made. He handed me the number for our HR representative and wished me the best. When I got back to my desk I called the HR rep. He reviewed the severance package and told me I needed to leave the building immediately. I said a few goodbyes to my colleagues and dropped off my corporate BlackBerry on the way out. Having just surrendered my only phone, I couldn't call my wife to break the news. I jumped in my car and drove to her office on the other side of town.

For weeks we had heard rumors of layoffs, so when I walked into her office she knew what had happened. We drove to a nearby park and talked about our future. She cried. I told her everything would be all right. My words may have sounded empty at the time, but I was confident things would work out for the best.

FOUR MONTHS EARLIER LEHMAN Brothers had declared bankruptcy, and I had struggled through much of the ensuing period. My job was saved by the Barclays rescue, but the financial crisis and global recession had worsened. I constantly fretted about the future.

I was one of 14 new analysts hired for the Silicon Valley office, a large number for a normal year. But this was no normal year. There had been several rounds of layoffs before I started, and Lehman's bankruptcy had thrown the markets into a deeper state of chaos. My peers and I had a lot of time to speculate about the future, and we wondered when the next bout of layoffs would strike. It was just a matter of time until some of the first year analysts were shown the door.

It wasn't just the concern of getting laid off that gnawed at me. The financial crisis had reduced deal flow, which had a direct impact on our office's revenue. Not surprisingly, our lack of deal flow affected the office culture and made coming to work far less pleasant. There was one associate I worked with, Eric, who made my life very difficult.

Eric and I worked on one project that was particularly stressful. The client meeting was to be held out of state on a Monday, and I spent the prior week getting the presentation materials ready. I checked in with Eric on a daily basis, hoping to get answers to my questions, but he was always too busy. The Friday morning before our meeting I printed the slide deck and dropped it off at his desk. I still had unanswered questions and needed his guidance. He promised that he would review the presentation and follow up with edits in the afternoon.

The afternoon came and went, but I heard nothing. Around 5:30 PM, I stopped by his office. The lights were off, and his coat was gone. Throughout the weekend I continuously checked my email, waiting for an update. Late Sunday afternoon I finally got a response: "Nathan, can you please come to the office now?"

I had fretted about this project all weekend, and it was time to finalize the materials. Eric was waiting for me, visibly frustrated and ready to pounce. He ripped into me, asking why the deck wasn't complete and why I hadn't asked for help earlier. I was ready to explain myself, but didn't get the chance. He shoved the marked-up slide deck into my hands and told me to deliver the final version to his house when I completed it. As he headed for the door, Eric yelled over his shoulder, "If you have any questions, get one of the other analysts to help you!"

The marked-up slides provided much clearer instructions than the ones he had given me earlier. I had a few questions on some of the slides and tracked down a second-year analyst for assistance. Around midnight, the courier picked up the final pitch books and delivered them to Eric's house.

This experience was typical of many assignments I worked on. While I knew what the job was like before I signed up, I wondered why there had to be so much friction. *Why did the other bankers need to make work so painful?* For me, the worst part about banking wasn't the long hours. It was the constant anxiety that came from knowing at any time, day or night, I might get an email requiring me to drop everything and head to the office.

SO, WHEN THAT FATEFUL January day arrived, I wasn't nearly as sad as I thought I'd be. I had been laid off. The worst had come, and there was nothing else to fear. I was ready to move forward.

While I initially felt calm, my new reality sank in the next morning. I woke up with no responsibility and nowhere to go. Time to find a job. I was excited to get started and optimistically thought it might take a few weeks to find my next gig. The financial turmoil had created a difficult environment for finance jobs, but I was confident I'd be fine. *Just work hard and every-*

thing will work out, I thought. But I would soon realize how difficult it would be to find *any* job in *any* industry.

A few days after getting laid off, I was surprised to receive an email from Eric. He encouraged me to keep my head up and introduced me to several contacts he thought would be helpful. I was impressed with his kindness. I left Barclays thinking he didn't like me and that he had purposely tried to make my life difficult, but I was wrong. I had been too quick in my judgment of him. In hindsight I attribute much of our difficulties to the high-stress, high-stakes environment our jobs created.

My first interview came two weeks later. Jefferies, a mid-sized investment bank, was looking to hire an experienced analyst. The position was identical to the one I'd just left, only with a smaller firm. I made it to the final round but completely botched the technical portion. The interview came to an end, and they told me they wanted to pursue other candidates.

The following week I got an unexpected phone call from Safeway, a grocery chain based in Pleasanton, California. Safeway was looking to fill a position in its corporate strategy group and the hiring manager invited me to interview. I was ecstatic but surprised they wanted to talk to me. I had applied for at least 100 positions and was only invited to interview when I had a relationship at the company.

At Safeway, I had no relationship and simply applied online. My background wasn't a direct fit for the role, but I was elated to be a candidate. The recruiting process taught me a lot about the company, and I hoped I'd get the job. As I wrapped up the final interview, the hiring manager asked, "I saw on your application you know Robert Edwards. Just curious, how do you know him?"

I told her that Bob was a family friend and I had gone to grade school with his daughter. Bob was currently the Chief Financial Officer of Safeway and would later be named CEO. Until this moment I had completely forgotten that I listed Bob as a contact when I applied. *So that was why I got the interview*, I thought. While I didn't end up getting the job, the lesson stayed with me.

While the economy was suffering during this period, there was a lot of buzz around clean technology. Venture capitalists had been pouring money into clean tech startups and many predicted that we were at the beginning of a clean tech revolution. These companies were rapidly hiring and I was hoping to find a spot. With the help of a few friends I made a list of 50 clean tech companies I thought were interesting. But when I visited their career websites I didn't find any openings that matched my background.

I was disappointed, but then I remembered a story my classmate Dave Lipkin had shared. When Dave was in his junior year, he wanted to find a good finance internship but wasn't gaining traction through job applications or traditional networking. He decided to cold email several corporate executives expressing interest in their internship programs. One of his emails was sent to the CFO of Bear Stearns who forwarded it to an HR rep. The HR rep likely thought Dave had a relationship with the CFO and invited him to interview. Dave ultimately landed the internship.

Like Dave, I hadn't been finding success with the traditional methods of recruiting, so I decided to follow his approach. I took my list of 50 clean tech companies and identified contacts at each. Sometimes I emailed executives, but most of the time my emails were sent to mid-level employees or the company's generic recruiting inbox. My email messages shared a brief background of myself and explained why I was interested in the company.

After sending out 50 emails, I anxiously waited to hear back, but nothing came. This strategy had taken most of the day, and I was tempted to write it off as a waste of time, but my opportunity cost was pretty low. One day I checked my email and was surprised to see a response. A director at Recurrent Energy, a San Francisco-based solar power producer, had an opening in his group and wanted me to interview for it. Unfortunately, I wasn't as lucky as my friend Dave. I didn't get the job, but I learned that when conventional recruiting methods aren't working, being creative and audacious can lead to new opportunities.

Over the next few weeks I was fortunate to interview for several positions. Before each interview I prepared the best I knew how, and thought I'd be a good fit at many of the companies, but each time I walked away empty-handed. I couldn't figure out why I was facing so much rejection. It was hard not to take it personally. *I must be doing something wrong*, I thought.

As the days turned into weeks, and weeks into months, it became apparent that I wasn't casting my net wide enough. I began applying for positions that had little connection to my degree or work experience. This led to additional interviews, but nothing seemed to work out. Despite feeling qualified for many of the positions, I was passed over for each one.

It was at this point that I hit rock bottom. I felt like such a failure. Doubt kept creeping into my mind and I wondered whether I'd ever find a new job. Until I lost my job, I didn't appreciate how much value I got from going to work. I missed having somewhere to go each day. I missed being a part of a team. I missed being needed.

Much of my identity was tied to my job, and when I got laid off, I felt lost. I looked for ways to distract myself from the rejection. Most weekends were an escape, but Monday would inevitably come, my wife would go back to work, and I would be reminded, once more, that I still didn't have a job.

Networking meetings and job applications rarely filled the entire day, and I had too much time to think about my plight. Several times I fell into a state of despondency, consumed by frustrations and discouragement. I tried to keep moving forward, and told myself that things would all work out. One day I had an epiphany. I was thinking about myself way too much. Constantly focusing on my needs and desires was only making the situation worse. I had been taught that the best way to forget my concerns was to focus on the needs of others.

I started looking for ways to serve other people and volunteered to organize service projects for my local church congregation. One experience stands out. It was a Sunday morning, and I was coordinating parking for a large church meeting. Our church lot was fairly small, and my job was to direct cars to the various parking lots nearby. A heavy rainstorm struck shortly before the meeting and lasted for several hours. By the end of the meeting I was completely soaked, but I had never felt better. Serving others had a cleansing effect on my soul and eliminated the selfish cares that were holding me down. Each time I did something kind for others, I felt better about myself.

I looked for additional ways to maximize my free time. Some days I went on long walks. Getting outside relieved much of the stress I was carrying. Other days I stayed in my apartment and read. I found reading therapeutic and drew strength from the lives of others.

I was inspired by people who had faced great trials in their lives but chose to maintain a positive attitude and not give up.

I kept a journal. Writing down my thoughts and feelings allowed me to compartmentalize my frustrations. Keeping a journal helped me find clearer solutions to my problems and enabled me to focus on things I could control.

Roughly four months into my search, I interviewed with Gymboree, a children's clothing company in San Francisco. After several rounds of interviews they extended an offer. The offer was in operations, not finance, but I didn't care. I accepted. Feeling excited for the new job and relieved that my search had come to an end, I was anxious to get back to work.

During my period of unemployment I interviewed with 65 people at 20 different companies. I had been rejected by almost all, but one of them said yes. And that was all I needed.

Lessons

When I got laid off, I felt like my career was permanently damaged. But in hindsight, it's an experience for which I'm grateful. I would never wish to relive that period again, but getting laid off and struggling to find a job taught me valuable lessons early in my career.

1) Never stop networking

I'm convinced that one of the reasons I got laid off from Barclays is that I failed to develop strong relationships with my coworkers. The slow financial markets created a less than positive work environment, and I routinely left the office as soon as my work was done. While other analysts discussed current events and the fate of the company with senior bankers, I mostly kept to myself. I networked when seeking the position, but failed to deepen those relationships once I started.

When a company needs to make difficult decisions, it's a lot easier to let go of people who aren't well known and keep to themselves. This may not be fair, but employment decisions aren't always clear cut.

There were other reasons for being terminated—my performance likely the main one—but failing to invest in relationships was a big factor. I've tried to avoid this mistake in subsequent jobs. Make the time to get to know your colleagues on a personal level. It's an investment worth making.

2) Show companies how you add value

Early 2009 was an awful time to be looking for work, but it's not fair to blame my difficulties on the financial crisis alone. One reason I couldn't convert interviews into offers was that I didn't show companies how I could add value. I thought companies would want to hire me because I went to a good school and worked for a good company, but that wasn't enough.

A good example comes from an interview I had at Gap Inc. During the interview I talked about my ability to analyze financial statements (my skill), but didn't demonstrate how that skill translated into helping them manage inventory more effectively (their need). Companies don't just hire smart people; they hire those who can passionately show how they will make an impact in the organization. Going to a top-ranked school, getting good grades, and even having exceptional work experience is not enough. Companies want to know how you can help *them*.

3) Don't just apply online

I grew up thinking that if I wanted a job, I should just apply and wait for a response. In fact, during high school, I spent almost a whole summer applying for jobs without getting a single interview. I finally landed a job when a friend referred me for an open position at his company, Blockbuster Video. For those keeping track, that's now two bankrupt companies I've worked for, but I digress. The referral immediately led to an interview with Blockbuster, and I started the next day.

My experience interviewing at Safeway is another reminder of the importance of relationships. Competitive positions get flooded by resumes, and it's tough to get an interview if your credentials aren't perfectly aligned with a company's need.

According to Dr. John Sullivan, a Silicon Valley HR thought leader, an average of 250 resumes are received for each corporate job opening. The most sought-after employers receive far more applicants. For example, Google receives 2.5 million applications each year, which equates to almost 7,000 per day. Do the math, and you can see that if you only apply online, you probably won't get the job. A "spray and pray" approach to your applications will likely fall short.

There's nothing wrong with applying online, but if that's your sole interaction with the company, you're doing yourself a great disservice. I've applied for hundreds of jobs, and I'm yet to get an offer without knowing someone on the inside. It's critical to develop relationships with prospective employers.

6

From Banking to Baby Clothes

Manager: "So how has your experience been so far?"

Me: "Things are awesome. I've enjoyed the company, and I feel like we have a great team."

Manager: "Good. If you don't mind, I want to share some feedback with you."

Me: "Absolutely. I'd love to hear how I can improve."

Manager: "Well, I've noticed that you get up from your desk fairly often. Why is that? Can you limit the breaks?

Me: "Yeah. I drink a lot of water, but, yeah, I'll try to take fewer breaks."

Manager: "Great, that's all. Other than that you're
            doing fine."

With that, my first one-on-one with my new manager came to a close. I had been at Gymboree for about a month, and for the most part, I was enjoying my role. A friend of a friend had told me about the Gymboree opening. After learning about the position and navigating through the interview process, I was hired. My new title was *inventory allocation analyst,* and I was responsible for making sure our stores maintained the right quantities of each clothing item.

I joined Gymboree for two reasons. The first was simple—I had no other options. It's hard to overstate how frustrating the job search had been, and I needed to get back to work. The other reason I accepted was more opportunistic. When I joined Gymboree, I hoped to leverage my financial analysis skills to help the company operate more efficiently. My goal was to come in, work hard, be an all-star, and get promoted.

One day my manager pulled me aside and asked if we could talk. It had been a month since our last one-on-one, and I immediately thought back to the discussion we had about my restroom trips. I left that meeting thinking, *Really, the only feedback you're going to give me is that I go to the bathroom too often?* I was tempted to take offense, but instead I tried to put myself in his shoes.

He was a first-time manager, and I was his only direct report. I may have disagreed with his managing style, but I believed he was trying his best. Thinking about my manager as a person, rather than as an object that was interfering with my progress, improved our relationship. We ended up getting along very well.

One of my initial observations about Gymboree was that the company culture was drastically different than what I had experienced in investment banking. It was a family-friendly environment, and most of my colleagues were incredibly nice. The work schedule was flexible, and I enjoyed working half-day Fridays during the summer. We had company "snack time"—remember, it's a children's clothing company—every day at 3:00 PM with free snacks in the cafeteria. As I enjoyed the daily snack time I couldn't help but wonder what my friends in finance would have thought.

The pace of work was also much slower. I was hired as a non-exempt employee, which meant that if I worked more than 40 hours in a week, I was eligible for overtime pay. This sounded great, but my manager made sure I never worked overtime. In fact, on several occasions he forced me to stop what I was doing because I had already worked an eight-hour day. This was especially frustrating when I was working on an important assignment and wanted to stay late to finish. My goal had been to exceed expectations, but these parameters made me feel confined.

The biggest challenge to my job was somewhat unexpected. As a retailer of children's apparel, Gymboree is in the fashion business. My colleagues frequently asked for my input on certain clothing patterns and designs, and I struggled to form an intelligent opinion. There were three reasons for this. First, I've never been interested in fashion. When I was a boy I would tell my mom to buy clothes similar to the ones my brothers' wore. Clothes never really mattered. The second reason was that I didn't have kids at the time. I was rarely around children and never thought about what they wore. Finally, I'm color blind. I struggle to tell the difference between certain colors, and since I've been wrong on so many occasions, I rarely describe things by their color.

These three factors made it tough to add value when our team was discussing a new line of clothing or trying to determine why some clothes sold more than others. On one occasion our manager took me and a few other analysts to a nearby Gymboree store. He asked us to walk through the store and guess which item was the highest seller in each department. I remember roaming the store in confusion. Did the "Happy as a Clam" shirt sell better than the "Daddy's Little Girl" tee? I had no idea. How was I supposed to know? Gymboree was a fine place to work, but experiences like this made me wonder whether I was a good fit.

I stayed busy the first few months at Gymboree and learned all that my role required, but after a few months I started getting bored. On a typical day I could complete most of my tasks in a few hours. Curious to see whether my peers felt this way, I reached out to Justin Decker.

Justin was the most seasoned analyst on the team, and we had developed a good relationship. While playing ping-pong during lunch, I asked Justin about his workload. He laughed, "Let's just say that if I only worked 20 hours a week I'd have ample time to get everything done."

"So if you're not that busy, what do you do with your extra time?" I inquired.

"I don't know," Justin responded. "I guess I just try to look busy. The days can get pretty boring. I wish I had more to do."

A few days later I asked my manager if I could take on more responsibility. In the past I had asked for additional work, but he usually dodged the question. This time his response was frank: "Sorry, I'm too busy to stop and explain what I'm working on. Just do a good job with your current assignments. You have enough on your plate anyway." Conversations like this made me wonder how long it would take to have increased responsibility.

The opportunity for promotion was also a concern. During my first six months at Gymboree, I had yet to see a colleague get promoted. I heard that all promotions were put on hold during the recession and wouldn't be discussed until the economy improved. I wasn't expecting a promotion anytime soon, but it worried me that our highest performers seemed stuck in their current positions.

Around this time I noticed that the financial markets had started to recover and several investment banks were looking for analysts. I still questioned whether I was a culture fit at Gymboree and I was concerned that I might not be able make a successful career in retail. With this in mind, I wondered whether I should consider opportunities outside of the company. But before looking elsewhere, I wanted to get a feel for how my manager viewed my performance.

I approached my manager and asked for direct and specific feedback. Formal performance reviews weren't scheduled for several more months, but I needed to know where I stood. He shared a few positive things I had done, and then said, "Generally, you appear disengaged. I like having you on the team, and you're a good performer, but you don't seem to take interest in your work. You need to become more passionate about what we're doing here." I thanked him for his feedback and our meeting came to a close.

While I was disappointed, I couldn't argue with him. I had tried to act interested and stay engaged at work, but it was a struggle. Not only did I feel underutilized, I just wasn't passionate about children's clothes. Gymboree was a great company, but I didn't connect with its mission. I knew I wasn't a culture fit, and I knew this would hurt my long-term opportunities at the company.

When I joined Gymboree, I thought that my investment banking days were behind me. I went through a lot during my time at Lehman and Barclays and didn't think I wanted to endure the banker life again. But my time at Gymboree made me think that finance was a better fit. I told myself that if I could just get through a two-year analyst program at a good bank, my career would be better off. I still wasn't sure what I wanted to do long term, but I was pretty sure it didn't involve fashion.

I aggressively began my job search and applied to several banks. I was fortunate to get an interview with Deutsche Bank, a former competitor of Lehman Brothers. After a few phone interviews, I was invited to interview in person.

I met with both junior and senior bankers, and everything went smoothly until my last interview of the night. I was scheduled to meet with an associate and second-year analyst. They walked into the room together and the analyst started asking questions. As I answered, I noticed that the associate, James, was completely disinterested. Glued to his BlackBerry, James refused to look at me. About 10 minutes into the interview he interrupted his colleague and spoke to me in a demanding tone: "Your experience sounds fine, but here's what I want to know. We're working a ton right now. Can you pull three all-nighters in a row and do perfect work?"

I didn't know how to respond. *Was he serious?* I eventually responded, unconvincingly, "Um, yeah. I can do that."

James shook his head in disappointment. "That's not good enough! Let's try this one more time. Are you confident you can pull three all-nighters in a row and do absolutely flawless work!?"

I declared, "Yeah!" almost shouting.

"That's a lot better," James responded, smirking with delight.

I walked out of the interview wondering what I was getting myself into. *Do I really want to get back into banking if my life is going to be that awful?* Fortunately, the decision was made for me. Deutsche Bank said no.

A few weeks later, I got a call from my friend Mike. We had stayed close since our internship at Lehman Brothers and were roommates during our final year at BYU. Mike was working at Piper Jaffray, a mid-sized investment bank. I learned that an analyst had recently left, and they wanted to hire an experienced analyst as soon as possible.

Piper Jaffray had a great reputation, and the culture, at least in the San Francisco office, seemed more congenial than other firms. I thought I'd be a great fit and forwarded my resume to Mike when we got off the phone. I made it to the final round of interviews, but they selected another candidate.

After several interviewing disappointments, a conversation with Tracy Black, one of the Gymboree executives, made me wonder whether staying in retail might make sense. Tracy and I shared mutual friends outside the company, and when I joined Gymboree she told me to reach out if I ever wanted to talk. I was now ready to take her up on the offer, and Tracy made time for me in her busy schedule. I wanted to learn about her background and discover how she became a top executive.

I learned that Tracy's first job out of college was at Famous Footwear. She was hired into the inventory distribution group at the company's headquarters in St. Louis, Missouri. Her starting salary wasn't anything to brag about (her words, not mine), but the area was affordable and she bought a house. Tracy quickly learned that she wasn't happy in this job and wanted to find a position in finance. She found a job as a stock broker, and planned to accept it, but she had trouble selling her home. Tracy stayed at Famous Footwear and decided that as long as she was at the company, she'd work hard and be an all-star.

Tracy went on to make major improvements to Famous Footwear's inventory management system. Her success led to multiple promotions, and after a few years she was recruited to join Levi Strauss & Co. in San Francisco. Tracy did well there, but still lacked passion for the retail industry. She considered buying and operating a few small companies, but she never pulled the trigger.

After a few years at Levi's, her manager was offered an executive position at Gymboree. Tracy had been the architect for much of Levi's allocation system, so her manager brought her along. Now only four years out of college, she was a director. One success led to another, and at age 41, Tracy was named as an executive vice president at Gymboree.

Tracy attributed her success to constantly seeking a better way to do things. She instructed me to avoid getting bored in my job, and said that people who get bored are usually boring people. "It's your responsibility to keep your job interesting," she said. Even though my job was more quantitative than creative, Tracy encouraged me to develop a passion and affinity for the product. She argued that it was important to look beyond the numbers and understand why certain clothes and accessories sold more than others.

I appreciated Tracy's candor, and our discussion was refreshing. I stopped applying for jobs and adopted a new attitude. I made a commitment to learn something new every day and put in an extra effort to understand Gymboree customers. This change in attitude led to improved job satisfaction and engagement. I thought, *maybe I can make a good career in retail.*

A month after my discussion with Tracy, I got a call from my friend Mike. It turned out that the analyst Piper Jaffray hired never showed up. Mike told me that Piper was inviting a few candidates to the office for a final round interview, and I was one of them. The interview was slated for the following week and the analyst hired would need to start immediately. I told him I was interested, but after hanging up I considered calling back and declining.

A few months earlier I would have jumped at the chance, but things had changed. My attitude had improved, and I was enjoying my time at Gymboree. But as I thought more about longer-term opportunities at the company, my concerns persisted. I knew that I owed it to myself to interview one more time. I went forward with Piper, and throughout the interview I had a strong feeling it was the right job for me. I wasn't thrilled about working 80-hour weeks again, but I knew this was the best career move. The next day I got an offer from Piper Jaffray, and I immediately accepted it. I was going back to banking.

I would be joining Piper's technology investment banking group in San Francisco. I would likely face growing pains as I jumped back into the finance world, but I was ready for the challenge. A new adventure awaited, and I was excited for it.

Lessons

1) Deciding when to quit

It's often said that people don't quit their job, they quit their boss. This isn't surprising since a direct manager has more influence over happiness at work than any external factor. Other reasons for leaving include: lack of career advancement, poor work/life balance, extreme boredom and inadequate compensation. For many, it's a combination of several factors that finally persuade them to jump ship. There's a lot of advice on this subject, but deciding when to leave your job is a very personal decision.

My biggest concern with leaving Gymboree was the fear of how others would perceive my exit. I had been at the company just under a year, and I was worried that future employers might view my short stint as a liability. Ultimately, my excitement for joining Piper Jaffray overcame these worries. Gymboree wasn't the right fit, and it was time to move on.

2) Don't underestimate culture fit

When I joined Gymboree, the company culture was an afterthought. But as time went on, I made mental notes of how management could improve the company. My list continued to grow, until one day I realized that management wasn't in the wrong, I was. Gymboree's leadership team had deliberately built a corporate culture to match the mission and values of the company. This didn't align with my ambitions and goals, but it did align with those held by the majority of Gymboree employees.

Research by Dr. John Bingham, professor of organizational leadership and strategy at BYU, shows that employees who strongly believe in the company's mission achieve greater success. These so-called, "true believers" are more likely to increase in status and influence than non-believers. Dr. Bingham's research is a great reminder of the importance of culture fit. When evaluating jobs, don't take the company's culture lightly. Invest time to understand whether you'll succeed and be happy in the new environment.

3) Become a Multiplier

As I think about my manager at Gymboree I can't help but think about the book *Multipliers* by Liz Wiseman. In *Multipliers*, Wiseman contrasts two different types of leaders—Diminishers and Multipliers. Diminishers drain capability and intelligence from their teams, while Multipliers amplify the abilities of others to produce better results. Diminishers hoard resources and underutilize talent while Multipliers attract talented people and use them at their highest point of contribution.

My Gymboree manager was too new in his role to apply one of these labels, but our interactions made me think about the manager I would like to become. Did I want to be a Diminisher or a Multiplier? As you interact with managers, think about what works and what doesn't. You can micromanage and focus on trivial behavior, or you can get the most out of your colleagues by investing in their development and giving them ownership for results.

7

Back to Banking

Tossing and turning, I finally rolled over and checked my alarm clock. 6:00 AM. *Dang.* I was completely exhausted but too anxious to fall back asleep. As expected, I was putting in long hours at Piper Jaffray, and still adjusting, both physically and emotionally, to the change of pace. The learning curve was steep, and the stress of the job impacted the rest of my life. When I went home from work I found it hard to unplug. Even on the occasional nights I got home early, I still couldn't sleep.

I had now been at Piper Jaffray for a few months, and despite my challenges I was performing well. I'd recently been assigned to work on an important M&A deal. The target company, which we were advising, was an emerging leader in cyber security that was running out of money. Investors had been pouring in cash for the past decade, and while the business had shown progress, it was far from becoming profitable. The investors had refused to put another dime into the business and wanted to sell the company to focus on more promising investments.

I had been staffed on the deal after one of our top analysts completed the two-year analyst program and joined a leading private equity firm. To date, most of my work at Piper had been helping tech companies prepare for initial public offerings (IPOs) or advising them on other capital raises. I had yet to work on an M&A deal, and I was excited, even a little nervous, to get my feet wet.

Since our firm was relatively small, the deal team consisted of only three people: a managing director, who had won the deal and managed the client relationship; a vice president, who led the day-to-day activities of the deal; and an analyst. As the analyst, I focused on the nuts and bolts of the deal, providing all of the analysis and creating client pitch books. While the culture at Piper was great, several colleagues had warned me about Jeff, the vice president on the deal.

Jeff called me into his office on a Friday afternoon and informed me that negotiations with one of the buyers had escalated. Both parties had agreed on basic terms and the deal would likely be announced in the coming weeks. Jeff instructed me to print a copy of both the current slide deck and summaries of the valuation models. I had been assigned to the deal just a few days earlier and assumed, rather unwisely, that all the files would be in good shape.

I reviewed the materials with Jeff and got a harsh scolding. Several analysts had told me of Jeff's short temper, but this was the first time I experienced it. He was mad that the documents were incomplete and demanded to know why I hadn't connected with the prior analyst before he left. I tried to explain the situation, but Jeff refused to listen. He mapped out how he wanted the presentation to look and described the Excel outputs he wanted to see. Finally, Jeff told me that this needed to be completed and on his desk first thing Monday morning. My heart sank.

I didn't know how long it would take to complete the assignments, but I knew I'd be in the office all weekend. *Are there even enough hours between now and Monday to complete everything?* I wondered. A quick calculation showed that I had about 60 hours to get everything done. I was already exhausted from a busy week and wondered if the assignment was possible. I sulked out of his office and got to work.

The weekend was brutal, but not as bad as anticipated. I completed most of the assignment, but even with the help of my peers, I struggled to figure out one of the analyses Jeff requested. I emailed him over the weekend asking for further explanation, but didn't hear back. On Monday morning we sat down to review the materials. Jeff, frustrated that it was incomplete, demanded to know why I hadn't followed his instructions. "Do you not know how to read?" he inquired, in a condescending tone. Having worked with difficult people in the past, I knew that responding to critiques like this would only make matters worse.

He sent me back to my desk with additional instructions, but I still couldn't figure out what he wanted. The analysis was very complex and I couldn't get the numbers to add up. I didn't want to tell him this, but we were on a tight schedule. I returned to his office and asked if he would come take a look. I walked him through the spreadsheet as he looked over my shoulder. Before I could explain why I was confused he asked, "I don't know why this is so hard. Are you stupid or something?" But as he reviewed the Excel model he went silent. After a few minutes he got frustrated and uttered, "Looks like I'll have to do this myself. Just email it to me and I'll take care of it."

Later that day I stopped by his office to see if he'd made progress. "I don't think we'll include this in the analysis," he responded. "It doesn't really add value anyway." He was trying to save face, but I knew he couldn't figure it out. I was tempted to say a lot of things, but simply nodded and walked back to my desk with a smile.

A week later the deal was announced and we threw a big party to celebrate. I was happy to have an M&A deal under my belt and felt validated by getting my first deal toy, a customized memento that marks the closing of a transaction. Going forward the workload didn't let up, but the almost debilitating anxiety that made my job so difficult had vanished. The work was intense, but I learned how to effectively manage my time and communicate with my superiors.

Banking was difficult, but there were a lot of things I loved about it. Attending client meetings was one of them. When Pandora, the internet radio company, was preparing to go public, our firm was considered as a potential advisor. I was the lead analyst on the team and prepared a presentation that explained why we were the firm of choice and how we would position Pandora for the IPO. At the last minute our managing director invited me to the meeting in Oakland. I got to meet the executive team and board of directors. Most managing directors wouldn't have invited someone at my level, and although we weren't selected as one of the advisors, the experience was memorable. I loved my team for allowing me to join them.

On one deal, this one with a company we were trying to sell, I interacted with the CEO and CFO on an almost daily basis. This kind of exposure forced me to be on my toes at all times, but I enjoyed working closely with an executive team. They viewed me as a trusted advisor and looked to me for assistance.

The most physically demanding stretch came during a three-week period when I worked over 100 hours each week. Several of the deals I was staffed on got busy at the same time. My schedule was crazy, but several of my fellow analysts stayed late to help me during this period. I'm still grateful for the sacrifices they made. We were a team and helping each other out was commonplace at Piper Jaffray.

Despite my busy schedule, I didn't get overwhelmed. Much of the stress I dealt with as a new hire had dissipated. My confidence had grown, and I took on new and challenging assignments in stride. Each new deal stretched my abilities and I was constantly learning new things. Additionally, I had developed a bond with the other bankers on my team. I was finally getting the investment banking experience I had wanted. I was happy.

When Summer arrived the hours became more reasonable. Senior bankers chased fewer deals as they took time off for vacation. Summer interns and a fresh batch of analysts had joined the team and they helped carry the load. I sat next to two of the new hires and enjoyed training and mentoring them. I wanted them to have a good experience and felt deep satisfaction as they developed new skills.

Summer came to a close, and I was chosen to lead analyst recruiting at BYU. I flew to Provo and interviewed a dozen undergraduate students who were trying to get into investment banking. I had been in their shoes a few years earlier, and I had a blast playing the role of recruiter. As a whole they were an impressive group and I selected several candidates for a final round interview. I came back to San Francisco energized, but when I walked into the office I could sense that something was wrong. It turned out there had been a major announcement while I was out of town. The head of our San Francisco group had been demoted, and a managing director in New York was our new leader. To make matters worse, three senior bankers had been laid off. In one fell swoop, the team I had come to love was decimated.

As expected, our former group head left the firm and over the next few months three more senior bankers followed him out the door. We were left with only one senior banker. While the mass exodus led to a significant improvement in my lifestyle, I was concerned about our group's future. With fewer senior bankers bringing in revenue, I wondered whether we might see layoffs. Not only that, but I missed the managing directors who left. At Lehman and Barclays, senior bankers had mostly treated me like a resource, but the Piper bankers treated me like a business partner. There was a feeling of humanity and camaraderie on our team, a rarity on Wall Street.

I was staffed on an IPO during this period and after the layoffs occurred I was the only one left on the deal team. One of the senior bankers in New York took over the deal, but he hadn't met the CEO of this company. There were only a few weeks left until the IPO, but we were concerned about getting kicked off the deal. At the next meeting I approached the CEO, reintroduced myself, and told him that our firm was committed to the deal and would make sure his company had a successful outcome. He gave me a confused look and said thanks. We didn't get kicked off the deal, and while It's unlikely my efforts made a huge difference, I'd like to think that they helped.

Time passed, and a new crew of senior bankers were hired to lead our group. They were recruited from bigger banks and brought a different attitude and philosophy. They made bold declarations about the team's future and promised we would experience great success together, but I had my doubts. Sure, the bankers came from prestigious firms, but most of them had less experience than the old Piper team. Even if the future was as rosy as they predicted, it would take a very long time to get there—big deals don't happen overnight. We'd likely spend the next year rebuilding the team's brand and trying to win new business.

Around this time I received great news—I was promoted to be an associate. Most analysts worked for two years and were then required to find a job elsewhere, but I had an invitation to stay longer term. I was flattered by the promotion, and considered staying in investment banking for several more years, but becoming a career banker was never my goal.

More importantly, my wife and I had our first child during this period. I didn't mind putting in crazy hours before, but when the new baby arrived I wanted to spend more time at home. Many bankers had successfully managed working long hours and taking care of a family, but I wasn't sure the sacrifice was worth it. My dad had always been around when I was a boy and I wanted to do the same for my children.

At this point most of my peers had left Piper to join private equity firms or hedge funds. Those jobs had always sounded intriguing, but as I learned more about them, they didn't feel right. I wanted to find a job where I could spend less time building financial models and formatting PowerPoint slides, and more time leveraging my interpersonal skills. I didn't know where I could find this, so I decided to stay at Piper until I had a clear idea of what I wanted to do next.

I tried to have a good attitude and welcome the new regime of bankers, but it was tough. The new culture differed drastically from the one I enjoyed. I started working ridiculous hours again and few of my assignments were interesting. Our team wasn't close to winning any deals and it felt like we were spinning our wheels. I wondered, *How much longer can I do this?*

Lessons

1) People trump position

During the interview process at Piper, one of the managing directors shared a great lesson. He had worked as a venture capitalist before moving to banking, so I asked him why he switched careers to join Piper. He replied, "I've found in my career that the people I work with are far more important than my job. It doesn't really matter what I'm doing, as long as I'm surrounded by great people."

I found truth in his words as I watched him and several respected colleagues leave the firm. Although I was doing the same work I had done at previous banks, my experience at Piper was far superior. We were a *team*. I felt like my colleagues cared about me. They invested in me and wanted me to develop. The demands were rigorous, but we worked hard together and succeeded together. Working with great people makes all the difference.

2) Ensure you have the right exit options

Exit options are critical if you aren't certain what you want to do long term. Having good exit options was probably the biggest reason I started my career in investment banking. But after a few years of experience under my belt, I found that none of the standard post-investment banking options looked very appealing. These jobs included private equity, hedge funds, venture capital and corporate finance.

Like my colleagues, I interviewed for several of these positions but didn't feel right about any of them. I had been climbing the investment banking ladder, hoping I'd reach the top, but I didn't stop to consider whether the ladder was on the wrong wall. Exit options are great, but take time to make sure you have the *right* exit options.

3) Seek stretch assignments

In his book *Flow: The Psychology of Optimal Experiences*, psychologist Mihaly Csikszentmihalyi talks about the need to match the right amount of challenge with the appropriate amount of skill. Too much challenge and you become frustrated; too little challenge and you get bored. When working on assignments just beyond your current abilities, you can experience a genuinely satisfying state of consciousness called *flow*.

It would be great if companies perfectly matched our assignments and skills, but this is very difficult in practice. I've frequently experienced flow at work, but most of the time I find myself at opposite ends of the spectrum—working on assignments that are relatively easy or tackling projects well beyond my current abilities.

The first few months at Piper Jaffray were a rude awakening. Each new project was a stretch assignment and forced me out of my comfort zone. It was painful, but I learned more during that period than the entire year before. I love the following quote from Yahoo CEO Marissa Mayer:

> "I always did something I was a little not ready to do. I think that's how you grow. When there's that moment of 'Wow, I'm not really sure I can do this,' and you push through those moments, that's when you have a break-through. Sometimes that's a sign that something really good is about to happen. You're about to grow and learn a lot about yourself."

It's the stretch assignments that expedite our personal development and help us experience meaningful growth.

8

Smile and Dial

It was 2:30 AM and we still hadn't made a decision. For the last hour the Piper Jaffray team had been debating whether to use 6% or 6.5% as the cost of debt in our merger model. *It was a model, a hypothetical scenario,* I thought. *Did it really matter?*

We were preparing a slide deck for a client meeting, and the managing director wanted to present several potential merger scenarios. It wasn't enough to simply discuss whether one company should buy another, we were expected to provide endless amounts of data to convince them it was a good idea. We finally settled on an assumed interest rate of 6% and called it a night.

After a few hours of sleep, I hurried back to the office and finalized the slide deck. Copies were printed, bound, and delivered to the vice president. He reviewed them quickly, joined the managing director, and headed for the meeting in San Jose. *Please don't be another worthless pitch book*, I thought. I hoped the meeting would lead to a deal, but I had grown skeptical. Our new team had been intact for several months, but we still hadn't won a deal.

During the past few weeks I'd spent much of my spare time searching for jobs. One path, private wealth management, was starting to look promising. Years earlier I did an internship with a team of financial advisors at Merrill Lynch, but I was so focused on getting into investment banking I didn't consider wealth management as a career option. Becoming a financial advisor would allow me to immediately begin interfacing with clients, something I enjoyed. The job was very entrepreneurial. I'd be required to find my own clients and provide them with an investment strategy catered to their specific goals. As a junior banker I had little autonomy in my work, and I longed for more control over my schedule.

However, the wealth management route had its drawbacks. New financial advisors had very difficult performance hurdles, including number of new clients (households with investable assets greater than $250,000) and total revenue produced. Most new advisors failed to reach these hurdles and were pushed out of the firm within the first year. I was confident I could be one of the few who made it, but it was still a risky path.

I attended an information session with Merrill Lynch where I met several successful financial advisors. The more I learned about the role, the more I thought, *I can do this. I can succeed!* I'd never worked in sales, but I had served a two-year proselyting mission in Oklahoma for The Church of Jesus Christ of Latter-day Saints, and experienced many of the same challenges that salespeople endure. I felt confident that through hard work and persistence, I could beat the odds.

After a few rounds of interviews, I got an offer from Merrill. They didn't give me a hard deadline, so I had time to evaluate my options. I thought becoming a financial advisor would be a good move, but I wondered what others would say. Most of my peers would likely question me for leaving banking to take a sales job. Many in so-called "high finance"—those working in banking, private equity, hedge funds, and venture capital—often looked down on those in private wealth management. But did it really matter what others thought?

BACK AT THE PIPER Jaffray office, the managing director and vice president returned from the meeting in San Jose. "How'd everything go?" I inquired. "What did they think of our pitch book?"

The vice president responded, "Oh, we had to make a stop along the way and then hit some traffic. We were late and only had a few minutes to talk. We weren't able to get to the pitch book. We left it with them and will follow up next week."

I nodded and exited his office, but I was fuming. *Unbelievable,* I thought. *We had worked day and night to prepare for this meeting, and last night we stayed at the office until 3:00 AM. And for what? So the senior bankers would show up late and not have time to present our work?*

For weeks I had been debating whether to leave and this was my confirmation. Everything had started to add up. I could no longer handle the frustration of working hard on an assignment just to have someone else botch it. I needed more purpose, and I longed for more autonomy. Additionally, I wanted to spend more time with my family. The next day, I called Merrill Lynch and accepted my offer.

I was nervous to tell my team I was leaving, but the conversation went better than anticipated. They wished me luck in my new role, and I left on good terms. I later reflected on my last few months at Piper and realized that my expectations of the new bankers had been unfair. They were a new group trying to build the best team possible. I had nothing personal against them and was happy to see the Piper team eventually find success amidst difficult market conditions.

I took a few weeks off before transitioning to my new position. This allowed me to re-evaluate my life. My busy schedule had prevented me from spending enough time on what was most important. I didn't want to lose sight of what made me happy and I made a commitment to spend more time on the things that mattered most.

I SPENT THE FIRST few months at Merrill Lynch in training. I was impressed by the training provided at the corporate level but found little support from experienced advisors. We were all on the same team, but there was little incentive to work together.

I knew I had to be proactive if I wanted to succeed, and sought to develop relationships with high performing advisors. Most had no interest in getting to know me, but I developed a friendship with one of them. "Since most new hires fail in the first year," he told me, "the senior financial advisors don't want to waste their time getting to know you guys."

I had signed up for a three-year training program, but found that most advisors didn't last very long. In fact, there hadn't been a graduate of the training program for over three years. One of the seasoned advisors believed it was the worst time to become a financial advisor. Competition from rival firms and online services was getting tougher each year. Cold calling—the prospecting method of most new financial advisors—was getting more difficult as various laws and "Do Not Call" lists stood in the way.

With these factors in mind, I looked for opportunities to join a team. I learned that Alison

Simon and Chris Bernard, two successful advisors I had briefly met, were looking for a junior advisor to join their team. After several discussions, Alison and Chris agreed to bring me onboard. Our team agreement had two main benefits. First, I could learn the ropes from successful financial advisors, but more importantly, they committed to make sure I successfully completed the training program. If I ever fell short of my performance hurdles, they agreed to make up the difference. This was a big benefit, especially in the short term. The agreement stated that all new clients we acquired from that point forward went into our new "pool," and we would split the revenue generated from them. The split wasn't completely even, but it seemed appropriate given my newbie status.

Once training was complete and I received the required securities licenses, my efforts shifted to the real work—client prospecting. Our team took advantage of the Silicon Valley location, targeting mostly executives and early employees at high-growth tech companies. There were hundreds of advisors pursuing the same clientele, but we were confident we could outhustle them. I used several prospecting methods, but most of my time was spent cold calling.

To no surprise, cold calling is traditionally one of the least effective prospecting methods, but it worked for me. I was self-conscious about my age, but on the phone nobody could tell I was in my twenties. Many advisors found success by leveraging friends and reaching out to family members. But I was always concerned that I might damage those relationships, so I mostly stuck to the phones. The rejection was immediate, and although people occasionally yelled at me, it didn't slow me down. I had faced intense and consistent rejection during my mission in Oklahoma. I was used to it.

Prospecting through cold calling was a numbers game, and I kept a detailed record of my stats. I learned that, on average, I spoke with only 12% of the people I called, and of that 12%, I scheduled a meeting 14% of the time. To get one client through cold calling, I placed 1,400 calls and held 23 initial meetings. So, if I wanted to win clients at a faster rate, I had two options. I could either improve my conversion rate by getting better at persuading prospects to become clients (something I was always trying to do) or I could make more calls.

Cold calling can be very intrusive, and a lot of people (including me) hate being sold to over the phone. I tried to be as polite as possible, but many HR reps demanded that I stop calling people at their company. Our branch manager occasionally got an angry call from someone complaining about me, but he knew I was playing by the rules. I may have annoyed people, but I never violated any laws.

On one occasion, I visited a software company in Redwood City. I had arranged four prospect meetings, and while Alison and Chris often joined for such meetings, I flew solo that day. My second appointment was with a software engineer. He was confused by my role and asked if his company knew that we were meeting. I reminded him of what we discussed over the phone—my team was advising several of his coworkers on their personal finances. But he had been under the impression his company hired me to deliver a financial training. I tried to clear things up, but he grew belligerent and walked out of the conference room.

The other two meetings ran smoothly, but as I walked out of the office I received the following email from an HR director:

Dear Mr. Tanner,

It has come to our attention that you are contacting Company X employees and requesting meetings with them to discuss their personal financial planning, and that you have used or intend to use Company X offices to conduct meetings with our employees.

Please be advised that under our Non Solicitation Policy, solicitation of Company X employees on Company premises, including parking lots, is expressly prohibited unless prior approval has been obtained by an officer of the Company.

In accordance with our policy, please refrain from any further contact with our employees on our premises and/or through use of Company email or telephone systems. We have alerted our employees that you are neither sponsored nor authorized by our Company to do so.

I was surprised that a company with over 700 employees would send a firm-wide email warning of a 20-something-year-old financial advisor. But that was enough for me. I never reached out to any employees at that company again. And for the record, there were no parking lot solicitations.

The most fascinating part of being a financial advisor was getting an inside look at people's financial situations. Those I had just met were willing to share intricate details of their financial holdings and they trusted me to help make important decisions. I was surprised that very few prospective clients had a well-thought-out retirement plan. Many looked affluent on paper (e.g. senior director, 20+ years of experience, expensive home, etc.), but had little in terms of savings and investments. They made a lot of money, but saved almost none of it. A good example of this was an executive at a successful enterprise software company. His salary was about $350,000, but he had almost no savings and was literally living paycheck to paycheck. Call me naïve, but I found this shocking.

Occasionally I met people who were in just the opposite situation. Despite never having a high paying job, some individuals had accumulated an impressive net worth. I respected them for their financial discipline.

After three months of cold calling I started finding success. I found one client that worked at a tech company that was weeks away from an IPO. She introduced our team to several of her colleagues and each became clients. They had sizeable stock options that were gradually liquidated when the company went public. It was a huge win for us, and I felt like I had made a big contribution to the team. Slowly but surely, my cold calling efforts were paying off.

Despite my success, I had a few concerns. Several software-based financial advisors had popped up and were growing rapidly. These providers were attractive to young tech professionals who preferred a low-cost, do-it-yourself approach. Our team charged an annual fee of roughly 1% of total assets under management, while most online advisors charged a fraction of that. Our team was a full-service platform that provided many services to our clients, but many prospects only cared about performance. They didn't value the intangible benefits we brought to the table. It was unlikely that a large client would leave us for a software-based advisor, but it was a growing threat.

My other big concern was cold calling. During my second year as an advisor I placed over 10,000 phone calls. Even though I was confident our team could help clients achieve their goals, my calls were intrusive, and I felt like I was harassing people. I tried a number of other prospecting methods, including networking events and asking friends/family for referrals, but I never felt totally comfortable doing those activities. I didn't like when others used my relationship to sell something, and I didn't want to do that to my friends. When the other finding methods didn't work, I went back to the phones. Cold calling had brought success, but it was starting to wear on me. Every time I picked up the phone it felt heavier.

I didn't ease up on my prospecting efforts, but my motivation had taken a setback. Going to work became less fulfilling and the boredom of making phone call after phone call was adding up. I was on a high performing team and my future at Merrill looked bright, but I wondered whether I was on the right path.

Lessons

1) Collect advice, but don't take it

Tom Peterson, one of my business professors, is fond of telling students to collect advice but not take it. His argument is that few people know you well enough to cater advice to your unique circumstances. But as we all know, that doesn't stop most from trying.

As a new financial advisor at Merrill Lynch I had to decide whether to join a team or remain independent. There was no shortage of advice doled out by seasoned advisors, and while all of it was given as gospel truth, most of it conflicted. I've found wisdom in my professor's words. Rather than getting annoyed when people tell me what I should do, I've learned to listen closely, thank them for the advice, and then decide if any of it makes sense for my situation.

2) It's not what you *make*; it's what you *save*

My observations at Merrill Lynch pummeled this lesson into me. Our team discovered that very few people accumulate wealth through salary and bonus increases. When income gradually increases, expenditures usually rise to match that increase. (For examples, google "pro athletes who are broke.") Most of our clients needed a big liquidity event, such as a company being sold or an IPO, to grow wealthy. Very few people have the desire or discipline to maintain a modest lifestyle as their compensation increases. I'm always impressed by those who can.

3) Don't leave your job without another lined up

It can be very difficult to find a new job, especially when balancing a busy work schedule. While at Piper, I considered leaving the firm so I could fully commit to my job search. I was working long hours and struggled to find time for recruiting. I bounced this idea off of a trusted mentor, and he strongly encouraged me to stay until I found something new. The lesson I learned from him, and from personal experience, is that it's a lot easier to find a job if you have one.

Sara Menke, the founder of a boutique staffing firm in San Francisco, says that having a job while looking for a job makes you that much more attractive to a potential employer.

> "Companies want to hire the best of the best and (those people) are usually employed… Quitting your job before having a job is a big risk that you should avoid. Most people do not have endless streams of income, so you should stay in your position until you get that firm offer for new employment."

If your situation becomes completely unbearable, you're probably wise to leave. Otherwise, consider staying until you line up your next position. It may be a struggle in the short term, but you'll be glad you stayed.

9

The MBA Decision

I had looked forward to this bike ride for quite some time. My dad was in town for the holiday weekend, and we were riding through the foothills of the Santa Cruz Mountains. I planned on a peaceful, scenic ride, but we'd spent the past 30 minutes discussing my career. I shared my concerns about the future, and my dad offered several nuggets of advice. He finally said, "Nate, I think you should strongly consider getting an MBA."

I thanked him for his input and reminded him that getting an MBA would be a waste of time and money. We got home from the ride and moved onto other activities, but I couldn't stop thinking about our conversation. *Maybe my dad is right*, I thought. *Maybe it's time to reconsider an MBA.*

As an undergrad, one of my career goals had been to get an MBA from a top-tier business school. Work experience and letters of recommendation would be factors for admission, but my score on the GMAT, the standardized exam required by MBA programs, would largely determine where I would apply. I started studying for the exam during my final undergrad semester and enrolled in a local test prep course. I took the GMAT once before graduating and twice a few years later when I was at Gymboree. I never reached my goal, but on my third attempt I received a satisfactory score.

With the GMAT behind me, the next task was deciding when to apply. I considered applying when I was at Gymboree, but most candidates admitted to top universities had worked three to five years. At that point I had only two years of work experience and thought I might be more competitive if I waited. Like many MBA hopefuls, the top ranked schools—Stanford and Harvard—seemed most compelling. But given my GMAT score, which was below their averages, my likelihood of getting accepted wasn't that high.

As time passed and I gained more experience, the idea of getting an MBA grew less appealing. Many in Silicon Valley argued that the MBA had minimal value. MBA grads were more prevalent than ever, and the degree, in and of itself, seemed less of a differentiator than in times past. The cost of getting an MBA made going back to school even less appealing. Tuition was rising dramatically and my opportunity cost increased each year. I kept an eye on application deadlines, and I often toyed with the idea of applying, but each year I remained on the sidelines. Several of my friends had been accepted to elite MBA programs, and I wondered whether going to business school made sense if I couldn't get into a top university.

When I joined Merrill Lynch I thought I had ruled out business school. I was in a career-track position, and leaving work to go back to school made little sense. I considered part-time programs, but I felt that classes would interrupt my focus. I was hustling and didn't need any distractions. But after almost two years at Merrill, I was reevaluating my career. *Do I want to be a financial advisor for the long haul? If not, is it time to pursue a different route? If I leave wealth management, what will I do?*

AFTER THE BIKE RIDE with my dad, I thought more about getting an MBA. The more I considered it as an option, the better it felt. Before talking to my dad I had felt trapped—none of my options looked appealing. But when I thought about getting an MBA, feelings of opportunity and hope came back. An MBA would allow me to leave the workplace for two years and re-evaluate what I wanted in my career. I would be exposed to many different paths and have the opportunity to do an internship between my first and second year. Eventually I reached the point when I felt ready to move forward. I had a new game plan.

I started researching schools and immediately faced a problem. It was early May and the deadlines for every MBA program had passed. I wondered whether one school on my list, BYU, might be accepting late applications. It had been five years since I completed my undergrad at BYU, and back then I didn't consider returning for an MBA. I had a great experience and loved the university, but thought I wanted a different experience for graduate school.

But as I spent time talking to friends who had received an MBA from BYU and heard about their experience, the option looked more appealing. I called the admissions department and learned that although the deadline had passed, they were still accepting applications. There were a few spots left, and I was encouraged to submit an application as soon as possible.

I now had two options. The first was to apply to BYU and, assuming I got accepted, start school in a few months. The other option was to wait until the fall, submit applications to a broader list of schools, and start an MBA the following year. I spoke with several trusted advisors, spent time researching the BYU MBA program, and decided to apply. I told myself that I would make a decision once I heard back from admissions.

In one very hectic week I completed the application. In addition to the GMAT, the application consisted of a resume, a statement of intent, essays, letters of recommendation, and a few other administrative documents. While waiting to hear back, I started investigating career paths. MBA internship recruiting started very early; if I were to go back to school, I needed to be prepared. I was interested in returning to the Bay Area after business school, so I reached out to local contacts for advice.

A lunch with Katie Mayfield at LinkedIn pointed me in the right direction. Katie had graduated with an MBA from BYU several years earlier. I was anxious to learn about her overall experience, but she spent much of our discussion talking about her HR career. She told me that BYU had a strong reputation in HR, and the *Financial Times* had recently ranked BYU as the #1 MBA program for Human Resources.

This was great, but most of my experience with corporate HR was filling out paperwork and sitting through compliance trainings. I was a big fan of NBC's *The Office*, and Toby, the soft-spoken, timid HR rep, had perpetuated many of the human resources stereotypes. I didn't want to become the next Toby.

But as I reflected on my work experience and what I enjoyed most in each of my jobs, I thought HR would be a good fit. I loved getting involved in recruiting while at Piper Jaffray and enjoyed analyzing the best way to train and develop people. I had worked on several dysfunctional teams, and I wanted to learn how to better establish a strong culture and motivate employees. Talking with Katie helped me learn that HR was more than just processing payroll and being the office cop. Human resources, when done right, was a strategic function to a business. Good HR professionals weren't paper pushers, but intelligent business people working to solve human capital problems.

Shortly after joining Merrill Lynch I read *The Start-up of You*, by LinkedIn co-founder Reid Hoffman and author Ben Casnocha. I found this book insightful as I considered my long-term career plan. The premise of the book is that all of us are entrepreneurs of our own lives. The authors argue that we can develop a competitive advantage by answering questions regarding our assets, our aspirations and the market realities:

A) **Assets:** What are you inherently good at? What do you have going for you? These can include soft assets (knowledge, skills, connections) and hard assets (cash, investments).

B) **Aspirations:** Where do you want to go in the future? What do you want to do? Who do you want to become?

C) **Market Realities:** What will people actually pay you for? Where is there a market demand?

As I thought through my assets, my aspirations, and the market realities, I felt like HR was the best route to maximize all three. While waiting to hear back from BYU, I spoke with as many HR professionals as I could find. Several of them were MBA grads and had moved to HR from other functions.

A conversation with an HR manager at Procter & Gamble was especially insightful. Like me, he had worked several years as an investment banker but discovered he was more interested in the human capital side of business—recruiting, training and development, employee engagement, talent man-agement, and compensation. He quit his job and enrolled in an MBA program, planning to transition into HR. As he shared his story, I felt confident I was heading down the right path. His story was my story.

By the time the BYU acceptance letter arrived, my decision had been made. I knew that BYU would be the right school for me. I accepted the offer and planned to pursue an internship in HR after my first year. I was making a huge career switch, but I've learned that it's better to have a specific plan and pivot as needed than to have no plan at all. My finance-to-HR switch didn't make sense to most, but it made sense to me.

At my previous jobs, most professionals at my level were expected to leave after a few years. But my job as a financial advisor was expected to be a long-term play. My team had heavily invested in me, and I felt bad leaving. They tried to talk me out of it, but my decision had been made. Leaving the comfort of a paycheck to pursue an MBA was a leap of faith, but I was confident it was the right move.

Lessons

1) Develop a competitive advantage

The Start-up of You teaches that we must act as the CEO of our career and take control of our professional future if we want to become globally competitive. To be competitive it's critical to understand your *assets* (what you're good at), you're *aspirations* (what you want to do), and the *market realities* (what people will pay you for).

Having only one or two of these isn't enough. You need all three to develop a true competitive advantage. I've often heard speakers say, "Find a job you love, and you'll never work a day in your life." This may be true for some, but blindly following passion can lead to an unsustainable career. I've found Hoffman and Casnocha's framework more practical. Know your assets and aspirations in light of the market realities and pursue a path that maximizes all three. Or, as one of my professors frequently instructs, "Find a playing field where you can win."

The next two lessons focus specifically on the MBA, but much of the content is relevant to other graduate degrees. Endless amounts of MBA advice can be found online, so I'll just share a few opinions on whether an MBA is necessary and how to decide which school is right.

2) Do you need an MBA?

Before deciding whether to get an MBA, it's critical to understand *why* you want one. There are many reasons for going to business school, but the most common include transitioning or advancing your career, building a professional network, and learning general business skills and principles. Even if one or more of these is important, it's wise to ask yourself if you can accomplish your goals without an MBA. Business school is not essential for everyone.

Making a career transition was my number one reason for going back to school. Building a network and learning more about business were factors, but getting exposure to different career paths and experimenting with those paths were essential. I loved having the chance to test drive HR. If my summer internship was a disappointment, I was confident that I could move back into finance or pursue a different path altogether. In addition to internships, good MBA programs provide students other experiential opportunities including case competitions and field studies.

If you're not looking to transition or accelerate your career, there's a good chance you can accomplish your goals without going back to school. It's a huge investment and your time and money might be better spent elsewhere.

3) Which schools should you consider?

Knowing why you want to get an MBA can help you evaluate which schools are right for you. At first glance, many schools appear quite similar, but as you dive deeper, the differences are more visible. Here are several factors to consider when evaluating schools: location, job placement and starting salary, prestige, specialties, class size, and tuition cost.

> **A) School location**. Many companies prefer to recruit locally, and while living in, let's say, Los Angeles for two years sounds awesome, you may face an uphill battle if you're trying to get back to Atlanta. There were several east coast schools I found appealing, but I was confident I wanted to live out west after graduating. Location goes beyond distance from future employers and includes weather, cost of living, and access to amenities.

> **B) Job placement & starting salary**. For most schools you can find a lot of data on job placement. What percentage of students have a job at graduation, and three months after graduation? What's the average starting salary by job function and geographic area? Into which industries are students going? It's important to answer these questions before making a big decision.

C) Prestige. In a mail survey of GMAT-takers at the University of Rochester, 750 respondents ranked their most important factors when deciding on an MBA program. Interestingly, *prestige of the MBA school* was twice as important as any other attribute. Prestige is certainly an important factor, but it shouldn't be the sole reason for selecting an MBA program. Too many students select a prestigious school without evaluating whether the program is a good fit. Don't let a school's ranking distract you from your goals.

D) Specialties. While some universities have a general management curriculum, others are known for being strong in a particular specialty, such as finance, marketing, or entrepreneurship. Strength of faculty can also play a big role when determining specialty. It is harder to measure, but some professors have a strong reputation and can be very influential throughout your MBA experience.

E) Class size. In this context, class size refers to the number of new students entering the program in a given year. Some top MBA programs admit close to 1,000 students per year while others schools are significantly smaller. A larger class size may enable you to build a broader network and select from a larger array of elective courses. A smaller class size may lead to more intimate relationships with your classmates and better access to professors.

F) Tuition cost. The cost of tuition can be a critical factor for MBA applicants, especially as tuition costs continue to rise. Several of the top MBA programs have an annual tuition cost of over $60,000. When you include cost of living and other factors, the bill for attending one of these schools can be almost $200,000. Many universities offset this burden through financial aid, but the cost may still be burdensome.

Once you learn which factors are most important, you can start researching individual MBA programs. There are many websites and online forums that can help. Current and former MBA students are especially valuable. I've found that most are willing to discuss their business school experience and answer questions.

As an undergrad student, prestige was the most important factor for ranking MBA programs. But as I grew in my career and researched the different business schools, my factors for determining the right fit became more practical. I wanted to attend an MBA program that would help me find a great job, I wanted to live in a location where my family would be happy, and I didn't want to take on any debt. The BYU MBA allowed me to achieve my goals, and I'm incredibly satisfied with my experience.

10

Finance to...HR?

The phone rang. I saw the number, recognized the California area code and immediately knew who it was. I'd been expecting to hear from LinkedIn for a few days, and this call meant the recruiting team had made a decision. My heart pounded as I uttered, "Hello, this is Nathan." My voice was so choppy I'm sure I sounded like a 12-year-old boy going through puberty.

Few things are more nerve-racking than answering the phone, knowing that the direction of your career is about to be determined. Sure, it was just an internship, but I wanted it desperately.

I was about halfway through my first semester of business school, and while I was swamped with six time-intensive courses, my mind was focused on one thing—landing a great internship. At this point I had received offers from two companies, but I was hoping to get one from LinkedIn.

LinkedIn had been my dream company since I started the BYU MBA program. I had spent the prior few months learning about HR and the many companies that recruited on campus. Most of them were Fortune 100 companies with an exceptional HR reputation. There was something to be said about joining a large company with well-defined roles and great training programs, but LinkedIn offered a unique value proposition.

The professional networking company had successfully gone public two years earlier and recently hired a new chief HR officer. In terms of both revenue and headcount, LinkedIn was growing like crazy and needed talented people to build a world-class HR team. Larger companies promised structure and a defined career path, but LinkedIn offered much more— the opportunity to develop and scale HR at one of the most successful technology companies.

Despite my passion for LinkedIn, I would have been foolish to focus all my efforts on one company, so I initially casted a wide net. Past experience had taught me that developing relationships was critical, and I spent a lot of time meeting professionals from various companies. Informational interviews (see Appendix A) taught me a lot about HR, and I learned which attributes companies looked for in candidates. I went through countless iterations of my resume and updated my LinkedIn profile on a continual basis. I have always hated mock interviews, but I needed the help—I had five years of finance experience and was rebranding myself as an HR professional. Mock interviews may have been painful, but there was no better way to simulate the interview experience.

I was so focused on recruiting that I fell behind in a few classes. I hated the feeling of coming to class unprepared, but I repeatedly told myself that I had developed a plan and needed to stick to it. Success in the MBA program, at least for me, would be determined by the job I landed, not my grades. I didn't come back to school to finally get straight A's; I came back to reposition my career and land a great job.

I was nervous when it came time to interview, but I felt prepared. By this point I felt comfortable explaining why I was making a career change to HR. I didn't have direct HR experience, but with the help of others I reviewed each of my prior jobs and identified HR-related assignments. For example, at Piper Jaffray I trained and supervised three analysts and led our internship recruiting efforts at BYU. Being able to draw on these experiences strengthened my rationale for moving to HR.

First round interviews were held on campus and each company had a different interviewing style. One company was very transparent about its process, and the interviewers told me in advance which questions they would likely ask. At another company, the interviewer tried to make me uncomfortable by asking, "If we hired you, how much money would another company need to offer to lure you away?" But for the most part I was asked standard behavioral questions including:

- Tell me about a time you dealt with ambiguity.
- Tell me about a time you used data to solve a complicated business problem.
- Tell me about a time you had to persuade someone.
- What are your three biggest strengths?
- Tell me about a time you dealt with negative feedback.

If I got through the first round of interviews, there was usually a final round held at the company's headquarters. But LinkedIn opted to have its final round over the phone.

I've always felt that interviewing in person is ideal. I like being able to see people face-to-face and read their body language. Unfortunately I didn't have this option, so I tried to make the most of it. I found a quiet room that was free of distractions and spread my notes across the table. Interviewers are easily distracted on the phone, so I kept my answers shorter than normal. Most importantly, I tried to bring a lot of energy and enthusiasm to the discussion. I spoke with three director-level professionals at LinkedIn, and each discussion was an additional confirmation that I wanted to work there.

By the time the LinkedIn recruiter called, I had been waiting anxiously for three days. When I answered the phone my heart was pounding out of my chest. My fate was about to be revealed.

"We want you to know that we were impressed with all of the candidates we interviewed," she said. My heart dropped, wondering if this was her polite way of saying no. "But we've made a decision. We're excited to extend you an offer to join LinkedIn."

I ARRIVED AT THE LinkedIn campus in early summer, anticipating a great internship. My first year of the MBA program was complete, and while I was thrilled to be working for my dream company, I knew it would be an adjustment. Most of my previous positions were highly structured, and while I had autonomy in how I spent my time at Merrill Lynch, there was nothing ambiguous about my objective—find new prospects and persuade them to become long-term clients.

Additionally, the LinkedIn internship would help me determine whether human resources was a function I wanted to pursue. While I'd been committed to HR since I entered the MBA program, I still harbored some doubt—it was such a drastic career change.

But a conversation with my manager put me at ease. We had lunch together on my first day, and I expressed my concern that I didn't have any real HR experience. "It's a valid concern," he responded. "And it's one I had when I first moved to HR. But all we're trying to do is solve business problems. It just so happens that we work in HR. Don't worry about it."

I was assigned one large project during the 12-week internship. Previous interns told me that their internship projects had been ambiguous, but I wasn't prepared for the level of ambiguity I would face. A summary of the project was provided, but there were few details on how to execute it. My manager made himself available to answer questions, but I was so overwhelmed by the scope of the project I didn't know where to start. *I don't even know what I should be asking,* I thought.

After a few days my manager answered enough questions that I could start moving forward. Unlike previous managers I'd worked with, he gave me a lot of autonomy and encouraged me to find creative ways to tackle my project. His confidence in me was em- powering. As time went on I felt more comfortable and took more intelligent risks. I learned to embrace ambiguity and found immense satisfaction in this role. I had never thought of myself as the creative type, but I enjoyed finding creative ways to solve the challenges of my project.

My colleagues proved to be the best part of my summer at LinkedIn. I looked forward to coming to work and seeing them each day. LinkedIn's positive momentum enabled the company to hire happy people who were high performers. My coworkers brought out the best in me, and I loved working on a winning team.

Additionally, LinkedIn's mission and values resonated with me. I have always been passionate about developing professional relationships and I believe in the company's vision to create economic opportunity for every professional in the world. This all may sound a bit over the top, but I can't say enough positive things about my summer. The internship surpassed my highest expectations and I felt lucky to be at such a great company.

The final week of my internship arrived, and I was satisfied with how my project turned out. I presented a summary of my work to the head of HR and her leadership team. The only thing left was a final meeting with my manager to find out whether I'd get a full-time offer. The offer came and I didn't need to decide whether I would accept. The past 12 weeks had already confirmed my decision—I would be coming back to LinkedIn.

ANXIOUS TO HIT THE road, I woke up early, packed my bags and started for Los Angeles. I had just completed my internship and was excited to be reunited with my family. The five-hour drive gave me time to think, and I reflected back on several of the experiences I had endured in my young career.

I thought about my internship at Lehman Brothers and the time I spent in New York. I thought about Lehman's bankruptcy, my departure from Barclays, and the struggles I had faced while looking for a new job. I thought about my experience at Gymboree, the growing pains of getting back into investment banking at Piper Jaffray, and the confidence I had developed through conquering difficult assignments. I thought about the highs and lows I faced at Merrill Lynch and the challenging decision I made to leave work to pursue an MBA.

Quitting my job to go back to school hadn't been easy, but it was the right decision. The BYU MBA program helped me find a great job, but the experience offered so much more. I thought about the essential skills and lessons I had learned in my courses, the professors who had inspired me, and the invaluable relationships I'd developed with my classmates.

Finally, I thought back to my summer at LinkedIn and the transformation I had gone through. The summer had confirmed my belief that HR at a high tech company was the right fit. I was overcome with emotion as I reflected on these experiences, grateful they had led me to this point. There had been many times throughout my young career when I felt confused and overwhelmed. Other times I felt like a total fraud. But at that moment, everything in my world seemed right.

I kept driving, filled with anticipation for what was in store. I wasn't sure where my path would ultimately lead, and though I knew additional setbacks and disappointments would arise, I was excited for the future. I knew I was heading in the right direction, and that was all that mattered.

Lessons

I discussed networking in previous chapters, but it's such an important skill it's worth revisiting. This time around I'll focus on networking when you need a job, and networking when you don't.

1) Networking when you need a job

As an undergrad student, as an unemployed job seeker, and as an MBA student, my networking had a very specific purpose—finding a job. When actively seeking a new position, it's critical to stay organized. I like to keep a spreadsheet that lists my targeted companies, professionals at those companies, the dates we spoke, a summary of what we discussed, and plans for following up. Having a system in place will keep you focused and allow you to track your progress. Consider setting a goal for your networking activities that will encourage you to remain active.

When looking for work, it's important to share your aspirations with friends and contacts. Having a compelling LinkedIn headline and summary is a great way to communicate to your network what you want to do in your career. If you're specific in your goals, your network can connect you with the appropriate professionals. Don't rely on simply applying online. Schedule informational interviews (see Appendix A) with interesting people in your network and ask for their advice. Try to meet with people face-to-face whenever possible.

2) Networking when you don't need a job

The best time to build and solidify relationships is when you *aren't* actively seeking a new job. Relationships develop more authentically when one party isn't wondering whether the other is only reaching out because they want a job.

When most of us meet new people, we often approach the relationship wondering what we can get from the other person. If you want to develop strong relationships, take the opposite approach and try to find a way that you can help that person. We all know that professional relationships are important, but the reward of networking often comes years down the road. Too often we let networking activities fall into Stephen Covey's "important but not urgent" quadrant and we never get around to doing anything.

One way to strengthen your network is to reconnect with old friends and former acquaintances. Staying active on LinkedIn will keep you informed, and you can receive daily insights about your network. Consider touching base and congratulating your connections when they have a work anniversary, receive a promotion, or accept a new job. But don't just network for the sake of networking. Make sure you are providing something of value to the person. It may be as simple as an article about something they are researching or a problem they are trying to solve. By adding value to them, you'll create a net positive relationship.

WHETHER YOU'RE LOOKING FOR a new job or just trying to strengthen your network, one of the most overlooked aspects of networking is the follow up. What's the point of putting yourself out there to meet new people if you're never going to talk to them again? Whenever I meet someone interesting, I try to add them on LinkedIn within 24 hours.

When sending a LinkedIn invite to someone you just met, or someone you don't know very well, I strongly suggest including a personal message. In your note, remind the individual how you met and share something memorable from your interaction. Personalized connection requests take a little extra time, but they humanize the networking process and strengthen your professional brand.

It's impossible to stay in constant contact with everyone you'll meet, but there are still benefits from having loose connections. You never know when you're going to need someone, and equally important, they don't know when they might need you. In fact, Adam Grant, author of *Give and Take: A Revolutionary Approach to Success,* points to research showing that we are 58% more likely to find a job through weak ties than strong ties. Why? We have a lot more weak ties than strong ties, and our weak ties tend to travel in different circles.

Networking, like anything else of value, takes time. The benefits may not be seen immediately, but that shouldn't prevent us from making it a priority. Networking can be very uncomfortable, and it may not come naturally, but networking is a skill that can be improved through consistent practice. Make a commitment to develop your networking skills.

Conclusion

One of my undergraduate professors had the following quote pinned to his door: "It is not the strongest that survives, nor the most intelligent that survives. It is the one that is most adaptable to change."

I remember walking by his office, reading the quote, and wondering why he put it there. But after Lehman Brothers went bankrupt and I was struggling to find a job, I realized why my professor felt so strongly about the need to adapt. Like Mike Tyson said, "Everybody has a plan until they get punched in the mouth."

The workplace has changed dramatically over the last few decades and will continue to change going forward. To succeed in the new business world, we can't rely on the stability of a linear career path within one company. To prepare for unexpected changes we need to continually invest in ourselves and make sure that we have a sustainable competitive advantage. We also need to invest in relationships and strengthen our professional network. Despite what goes on around us, we are in charge of our own fate, and we must manage our careers proactively.

FINALLY, I'D LIKE TO share some of the best career advice I've received as a young professional. Consider applying these five lessons as you launch and grow your career.

1) Balance deliberate and emergent strategies

In his book, *How Will You Measure Your Life?*, Clayton Christensen discusses the differences between deliberate and emergent strategies. In your career, a deliberate strategy is the specific plan you craft for your future, while an emergent strategy is a realized pattern that wasn't expressly intended. In other words, an emergent strategy is the path you take after your circumstances have changed.

It's wise to have a plan, but Christensen believes too many young people stress about their future and think they're supposed to "have their careers planned out, step-by-step, for the next five years. High-achievers, and aspiring high-achievers, too often put pressure on themselves to do exactly this. . .But having such a focused plan really only makes sense in certain circumstances." Christensen continues:

"If you haven't reached the point of finding a career that (is right for you), then, like a new company finding its way, you need to be emergent. This is another way of saying that if you are in these circumstances, experiment in life. As you learn from each experience, adjust. Then iterate quickly. Keep going through this process until your strategy begins to click. As you go through your career, you will begin to find the areas of work you love and in which you will shine...Strategy almost always emerges from a combination of deliberate and unanticipated opportunities. What's important is to get out there and try stuff until you learn where your talents, interests, and priorities begin to pay off."

2) Pursue what you're constantly thinking about

Henry Eyring, a former professor at the Stanford Graduate School of Business, tells the story of how he ended up studying business management. His father was a renowned chemist who taught at Princeton University and hoped his son Henry (known as "Hal" among family and friends), would follow in his footsteps. Eyring tells the following story.

"My father was (teaching physics) at a blackboard we kept in the basement...Suddenly he stopped. 'Hal,' he said, 'we were working at this same kind of problem a week ago. You don't seem to understand it any better now than you did then. Haven't you been working on it?'"

Eyring admitted he had not. "You don't under-stand," his father went on. "When you walk down the street, when you're in the shower, when you don't have to be thinking about anything else, isn't this what you think about?"

"When I told him no," Eyring concludes, "my father paused...then said, 'Hal, I think you'd better get out of physics. You ought to find something that you love so much that when you don't have to think about any-thing, that's what you think about.'"

I love this story and the sage advice given by Eyring's father. Finding passion in the workplace may not come immediately. Make an investment to learn what you're passionate about and look for opportuni-ties to pursue what you love.

3) Find mentors

A good mentor functions as a role model and provides support and encouragement to a less experienced employee. Many companies have a formal mentoring program and assign a mentor when new hires join the company, but too often these forced relationships fail to accomplish the program's goals.

For example, during my internship at Lehman Brothers, I was assigned a formal mentor. My mentor was a senior banker in a different group and was too busy to meet with me. I didn't hear from him until the last week of my internship when he invited me for a last minute steak lunch. The food was amazing, but the experience was awkward. I knew he didn't really want to be there, and I didn't know what questions to ask.

The best mentoring relationships develop organically. If you find someone you admire and want to learn from, schedule a time to ask for their advice. If the discussion goes well and you sense a connection, ask if they'd be willing to chat again in the future. Don't formally ask them to be your mentor. Doing so may make the relationship uncomfortable. There's no need to force it.

One of my professors, Dr. Troy Nielson, encourages having several mentors inside and outside your current company. He lists several benefits of having a mentor within your company:

- Faster promotions and opportunities for advancement
- Learning "unwritten rules" of the company
- Salary growth
- Learning and skill development
- Increased job satisfaction

Having mentors outside your company is also important. These mentors are often more objective and can help you evaluate new job opportunities. The best mentors are invested in your success and will give you honest and candid feedback. The professionals you'd like to have as a mentor are likely very busy, so it's your responsibility to drive the relationship.

4) Focus on strengths

While many spend their efforts focused on developing weaknesses, performance guru Marcus Buckingham argues that top performers excel not by focusing on their deficiencies, but their strengths. According to Buckingham, "Your strengths are the work (or school) activities that consistently make you feel productive, energized, and engaged." It's not enough to simply be good at something, you also need to enjoy the activity.

As a young professional, you're unlikely to have full autonomy over your schedule. But finding a way to leverage your strengths in the workplace will make you happier and more successful. Before making your next career move, reflect on the activities that leave you energized. Try to find a position where you can play to your strengths.

5) Commit to a life of learning

One of my favorite professors, Dr. Steve Albrecht, started each class period by sharing a life lesson and regularly encouraged us to commit to a life of learning. On the last day of class Dr. Albrecht said, "If you leave here with only one thing from this class, I hope you'll leave having committed yourself to a consistent reading program." He then outlined the five elements of his reading program:

1) Current events

2) General business news
3) Industry-specific news
4) Leisure reading
5) Spiritual reading

Albrecht believes that these five elements will help you stay knowledgeable, interesting, and centered on what's most important.

Committing to a life of learning goes beyond just reading. For those not in school, free courses are available online through Massive Open Online Courses (MOOCs). Coursera, Udacity, and Khan Academy are a few of the larger MOOC providers and offer courses from some of the most prestigious universities in the world.

Last year I was interested in learning basic computer programming skills and was impressed with the online offerings I found. MOOCs are a great way to self-educate and are available to anyone with an internet connection. Don't let your education stop when you finish school. Commit to a life of learning.

I'VE INCLUDED TWO APPENDICES you may find helpful. Appendix A is a brief guide that teaches how to hold effective informational interviews—a critical part of networking. Appendix B lists my favorite books that are relevant to students and young professionals. If you'd like to connect or have any questions, feel free to email me at nhtanner@gmail.com or follow me on Twitter at @nhtanner. I'd love to hear from you.

Appendix A

Informational Interviews

Do you want to get really good at networking and build strong relationships with potential employers? If so, learning how to master informational interviews is a great place to start.

What is an informational interview?
An informational interview is a meeting in which potential job seekers get advice on their careers, the industry, and/or the corporate culture of a potential future workplace. During the discussion, the employed professional is learning about the job seeker and judging their professional potential and fit with the corporate culture. To be clear, info interviews are not job interviews. A better name for them is probably *informational discussions,* but I'll stick to info interviews for now.

Your purpose during an info interview is three-fold:

1) Build a new relationship and make a good impression
2) Learn about the company
3) Find additional people to speak with

You may not know exactly what you want to do, but taking time to figure out your career goals in advance will make your informational interviews far more effective.

Create a list of professionals to contact

I'll soon jump into specifics of how to make a successful informational interview, but let's first discuss how to find the right individuals to call. For many, this is the most difficult part.

Build a company list

The first step is to make a list of companies. If you're a student, find out which companies recruit on campus or recently hired students from your school. It's a good place to start, but don't limit yourself to that list. Next, think about all the companies where you'd love to work. At this point, don't rule out companies you think might be "out of your league." The best thing about informational interviews is that you are gathering *information*—you aren't asking for a job. A quick conversation with a professional at your dream company will help you gauge the likelihood of getting hired.

If you've already spent time in the workplace, you may already have a good list. But If you're still struggling to find companies, jump on Google and search for companies by your preferred industry or location. Get creative in your queries.

There's no limit to the number of companies you can include in your initial list. However, you'll likely get overwhelmed if you're trying to contact people at more than 20 companies. Start with your top five and go from there.

Identifying individuals using LinkedIn

The next step is to identify the right professionals at your preferred companies. LinkedIn is the best place to start. Some of you may find this section elementary, so feel free to skip ahead.

Let's assume you're a marketing student or professional and Honeywell is on your list. In the LinkedIn search bar (top of the screen), type in "Honeywell" and select the "Companies" option.

On the right hand side you'll find a section called "How You're Connected" that shows how you're connected to professionals at this company. As of this writing, there are three groups of people: first-degree connections, second-degree connections, and the total number of employees at the company. If you don't have first- or second-degree connections, you will only see the number of employees who are on LinkedIn.

First-degree connections are people that you already know. Or, I should say, you ought to know, because at one point you accepted their connection request. Assuming you have first-degree connections, you can view them by clicking on the number just left of "first-degree connections."

If you click on the profile of a first-degree connection, you can view their background and details about their current position. Below their profile photo is the option to view "Contact Info." Most professionals will have an email address listed here. While LinkedIn messages are very effective, I've found that most people respond faster to emails.

If you have first-degree connections at a company on your list, consider emailing them to schedule an informational interview (I'll discuss this later in the section). If you know this person well but they don't work in your desired function, consider asking for an introduction.

Second-degree connections are people who are connected to your first-degree connections. You may not know them, but one of your immediate connections does. Go back to the "How You're Connected" section on the company's page and click on the number just left of "second-degree connections." This takes you to a list of second-degree connections. You'll notice that under each person's job title you can see your shared connections.

If you feel comfortable, ask your shared connection to introduce you to the second-degree connection. You can do this in LinkedIn by hovering over the arrow button just to the right of the blue "Connect" box, then clicking "Get Introduced." Sometimes it's preferred to email your shared connection and ask for an introduction. Various scripts can be found online by searching "email introduction."

LinkedIn Alumni Tool

Another method for finding the right people to contact is the LinkedIn Alumni Tool. To access this tool, go to the home page, hover over "Connections" and select "Find Alumni."

From the Alumni Tool, you can perform a search for graduates from your school. Criteria for this search may include location, company, job function, or graduation date. You also have the option to change universities, which may be helpful if you have ties to a university you didn't attend.

The Alumni Tool is especially valuable for those who want to work in a specific location or job function. For example, if you're interested in marketing and want to work in the Dallas/Fort Worth area, you can quickly narrow your list to only include alumni that match your preferences.

Once you've selected your criteria, scroll down and view the individuals. If there is an envelope below the job title, it's a first-degree connection and you can message or email them. If you see a professional's silhouette and a plus sign below the job title, this is not a first degree connection. Look in the bottom right of their profile photo. If there is a Venn diagram, hover over it to see the connections you have in common.

If you don't have mutual connections but still want to connect with an individual, there are two options. First, see if your school has an alumni database on its website. This can be a great place to find contact information. The other option is to send the individual a personalized connection request. In the message, be polite and briefly explain your reasons for wanting to connect. You may find that the professional accepts your invitation but doesn't respond. If this happens, consider sending a more detailed LinkedIn message or email. Once you're connected you can find their email address under the "Contact Info" section of their profile.

Summary
Now that you have a list of individuals you'd like to meet with, let's discuss the steps for making a successful informational interview.

Six steps for a successful info interview

The following steps were created from several discussions with current and former MBA students. Much of the advice is opinion, but it's a great place to start.

1) Scheduling the info interview

In your initial email, provide a one-sentence summary of yourself, share why you want to speak, and request a few minutes (consider asking for 15-30 minutes) of their time to ask questions about their company and work experience. Make sure you make it clear you're asking for advice and not a job. Thank them in advance for any time they can share. They are very busy, so be flexible with your schedule. Here's a sample email:

Hi Steve,

My name is Chris Richards, and I'm a sophomore studying marketing at UT-Austin.

I'm really interested in brand management and wanted to learn more about your experience at General Mills. When convenient, would you be open to answering a few of my questions?

Many thanks,
Chris

2) Preparation

One you've scheduled the interview, it's time to prepare. Failing to prep for informational interviews wastes everyone's time and can damage your personal brand. Take time to learn about the professional and his or her company.

Researching the company
It's helpful to know what products and services the company offers, information about the CEO, and what he or she has said recently, as well as basic information about the function (e.g. marketing, finance, etc.) in which you'd like to work. You don't need to memorize the details of the company's cash flow statement, but a little research will convey genuine interest and improve the quality of your conversation.

Researching the individual
LinkedIn profiles can tell you a lot. Don't ask questions you can easily answer by glancing at their profile. A general rule of thumb is that if something is listed on a LinkedIn profile, it's fair game to bring up in a professional way.

3) Starting the info interview
Here's a general outline I followed during MBA recruiting.

- Thank them for their time.
- Remind them that you planned to chat for 15 minutes (or whatever time you said in the email), and ask if that is still okay.

- Share your objective for the call (learn more about the company, get to know them, ask about life inside the company, etc.).
- Say something along the lines of, "Before I ask a few questions, would it be helpful if I shared a little about myself?" They'll likely say yes. This is your opportunity to provide a *very brief* summary of your background. Sharing a little about yourself allows the professional to get to know you better and tailor the responses to your situation.

Remember, you're the one driving the conversation. It's your responsibility to make sure they are engaged.

4) Possible questions to ask

While your goal may be to find a job, that isn't the goal of this phone call. You're trying to build a relationship and gather information. Several of these questions are fairly generic. The more research you've done, the better questions you can ask.

- Can you tell me about your background and how you ended up at your current company?
- What qualities or skills have made you successful?
- What does a typical day look like for you?
- What qualities do you look for when hiring a candidate?

- How has your experience differed from expectations? (This is especially good if they are a junior employee or recently joined the company.)
- How do your company's values influence how people make decisions? (Only ask if they have very defined corporate values. Consider asking about one of the specific values.)
- If you were in my shoes, what would you do to prepare for a potential job or internship with your company? (Good question if you know they are hiring.)
- Reference something on their LinkedIn profile (don't be creepy) and ask a specific question, such as, "I saw on your LinkedIn profile that you were at Procter & Gamble before joining Adobe. How was the transition from CPG to tech?"
- I read that… (tell them something interesting you've learned about the company). Can you tell me more about that?
- Is there anyone else I can speak with at your company to learn more about (fill in the function you're interested in)?
- Do you have any final pieces of advice for someone in my shoes?

5) Ending the info interview

When the allotted time has passed, tell them you want to be respectful of their time and wrap up the call. Never go long unless they specifically say it is okay. Thank them again and tell them you would love to keep in touch. Ask if you can follow up if you have more questions.

6) Follow up

Don't forget to follow up! Send them a hand-written note or email expressing gratitude. In the note, reference something you discussed that was insightful. If they helped you get a job or introduced you to someone else, follow up with an update. People love to hear how they've been helpful! Following up will further strengthen the relationship. If you had a good conversation and want to stay in touch, send an invitation to connect on LinkedIn.

Common mistakes to avoid

Below is a list of mistakes to avoid when making informational interviews.

- Don't let your first info interview be with someone fairly high up at a company. Practice an info interview with a friend, classmate, or contact who knows you well. After a few info interviews you'll feel a lot more comfortable and will likely ask better questions.

- When you begin the call, don't start rambling about yourself. Make sure that your introduction is brief. The focus is on asking good questions and learning from them, not "pitching" yourself.

- As mentioned earlier, don't ask questions you can easily answer by doing simple research. It will make you sound lazy. *The more specific questions you can ask, the better conversation you'll have and the better impression you'll leave.*

- Avoid telling professionals that you're "just trying to learn about a lot of companies." This is your chance to express interest in *their* company!

- Don't be too mechanical. Be professional, but try to have fun during the discussion. Companies aren't interested in hiring robots. Try to sound energetic and engaging.

- If you haven't met someone, or don't know them very well, don't add them to LinkedIn without including a personalized connection request.

Track everything

Take notes during your conversations. You'll be surprised at how much you forget in a short period of time. During MBA recruiting I took a picture of my notes after each call and saved them in a folder marked *Info Interviews*. This allowed me to go back and reference the notes before interviews and future interactions. Come up with a system that works best for you.

Summary

In short, be courteous, do research, ask informed questions, don't go over your scheduled time without permission, tell them thanks, and follow up.

Appendix B

Recommended Reading

Here are 20 of my favorite books that are relevant to students and young professionals. While several of them are not traditional business books, I believe anyone pursuing a career in business will find them valuable. Many of these summaries have been adapted from those provided by the authors and reviewers.

Drive: The Surprising Truth About What Motivates Us
BY DANIEL H. PINK

Pink argues that there's a gap between what science knows about motivation and what business does. Our current business operating system—which is built around external, carrot-and-stick motivators—doesn't work and often does harm. He suggests a new approach to motivation that has three essential elements:

1) **Autonomy**: the desire to direct your own life
2) **Mastery**: the urge to get better and better at something that matters
3) **Purpose**: the yearning to do what you do in the service of something larger than yourself

Eat Move Sleep: How Small Choices Lead to Big Changes
BY TOM RATH

Tom Rath is the author of *StrengthsFinder 2.0*, *How Full is Your Bucket?*, and other bestselling business books. As the title *Eat Move Sleep* suggests, Rath discusses how our eating, moving, and sleeping habits can have a big impact on how we operate as professionals. He offers over 100 practical suggestions that can be implemented immediately. My biggest takeaway was the negative impact of sitting. Reading about this motivated me to use a standing desk whenever possible.

Essentialism: The Disciplined Pursuit of Less
BY GREG MCKEOWN

We constantly hear others "humble brag" about how busy they are and how many things they need to accomplish. McKeown argues that it's time to focus on doing less while accomplishing more. After reading this book I re-evaluated my priorities and learned to say "no" more often. As McKeown says:

"Essentialism is not about how to get more things done; it's about how to get the right things done...It is about making the wisest possible investment of your time and energy in order to operate at your highest point of contribution by doing only what is essential."

The Hard Thing About Hard Things

BY BEN HOROWITZ

Ben Horowitz, successful entrepreneur and cofounder of Andreessen Horowitz, offers practical advice on building and running a startup. While his advice is directed to entrepreneurs, the lessons are applicable to all in the business world. His book tackles topics such as how to lay people off, why workplace training is flawed at most companies, and how to balance accountability and creativity. *The Law of Crappy People* is my favorite lesson. It states that, "For any title level in a large organization, the talent on that level will eventually converge to the crappiest person with the title."

Peter Thiel's *Zero to One: Notes on Startups, or How to Build the Future* is also a great read. Thiel provides insights into innovation and entrepreneurship which are applicable for those launching a career.

How Will You Measure Your Life?

BY CLAYTON CHRISTENSEN

Originally given as a Harvard Business School commencement address and later expanded into a book, Clayton Christensen's *How Will You Measure Your Life?*

offers a series of guidelines for finding meaning and happiness in life. It's a great read for anyone seeking to balance a successful career and a fulfilling life. Here's my favorite quote:

> "You can talk all you want about having a clear purpose and strategy for your life, but ultimately this means nothing if you are not investing the resources you have in a way that is consistent with your strategy."

How to Win Friends and Influence People
BY DALE CARNEGIE

Originally published during the Great Depression, Dale Carnegie's book is a classic that has withstood the test of time. I read this book as an undergrad and have been trying to apply its principles ever since. While many argue his advice is simply common sense, I find it very valuable since building relationships never came naturally to me. Here are my favorite takeaways:

- To be interesting, be interested.
- Remember that a person's name is to that person the sweetest and most important sound in any language.
- Be a good listener. Encourage others to talk about themselves.
- If you want to gather honey, don't kick over the beehive.
- You can make more friends in two months by becoming interested in other people than you

can in two years by trying to get other people interested in you.

John Adams

BY DAVID MCCULLOUGH

I'm a huge fan of biographies and *John Adams* is one of my favorites. Adams was a polarizing figure throughout the American Revolution and held vicious grudges with several of the Founding Fathers. Despite his many flaws, Adams provided consistent leadership and played a critical role during the founding of the United States.

Biographies help me gain insights into how successful people handle crises, solve complex problems, and pursue interesting careers. Other favorite historical biographies include *Truman* (also by McCullough), *Benjamin Franklin: An American Life* (by Walter Isaacson) and *Alexander Hamilton* (by Ron Chernow).

Man's Search for Meaning

BY VICTOR FRANKL

Man's Search for Meaning is one of the few books I've read multiple times. Frankl's account of life in a concentration camp is both heartbreaking and inspiring. Frankl persuasively argues that people are motivated more by meaning than pleasure or happiness. Here's my favorite quote: "Suffering ceases to be suffering the moment it finds a meaning."

I first read this book shortly after getting laid off from Barclays. Reading it provided perspective on my personal trials and reminded me that I needed to find meaning outside of the workplace.

The Millionaire Next Door
BY THOMAS J. STANLEY

In *The Millionaire Next Door*, Stanley summarizes his research into the key characteristics that explain how Americans become wealthy. His research shows that many who live in expensive homes and drive luxury cars do not actually have much wealth. Here are five of the "common denominators" among those who successfully build wealth:

- They live well below their means.
- They allocate their time, energy, and money efficiently and in ways conducive to building wealth.
- They believe that financial independence is more important than displaying high social status.
- Their parents did not provide economic outpatient care.
- Their adult children are economically self-sufficient.

As a financial advisor, I was surprised by how many people with large incomes had accumulated little wealth. The principles of this book are simple to understand, but too often ignored.

Mindset: The New Psychology of Success
BY CAROL DWECK

Mindset came highly recommended by my first manager at LinkedIn. The central message of the book is that your mindset, or the view you adopt for yourself, profoundly affects the way you live your life. A fixed mindset comes from the belief that your qualities are carved in stone—who you are is who you are, period. A growth mindset comes from the belief that your basic qualities are things you can cultivate through effort. Having a growth mindset encourages effort and learning.

Multipliers: How the Best Leaders Make Everyone Smarter
BY LIZ WISEMAN

Why do some leaders (Diminishers) drain capability and intelligence from their teams, while others (Multipliers) amplify it to produce better results? Wiseman provides insight into how leaders should focus less on being geniuses and more on becoming genius makers. My favorite quote in *Multipliers* comes from U2's Bono:

> "It has been said that after meeting with the great British Prime Minister William Ewart Gladston, you left feeling he was the smartest person in the world; but after

meeting with his rival Benjamin Disraeli, you left thinking you were the smartest person."

Wiseman's latest book, *Rookie Smarts: Why Learning Beats Knowing in the New Game of Work*, effectively teaches how experience can be a curse and why people coming into a new role frequently outperform those with more experience.

Never Eat Alone

BY KEITH FERRAZZI

Never Eat Alone is the bible for building professional relationships. Below are my three favorite lessons:

- *Build your network before you need it.* The best networking isn't networking at all. Your goal should be to build relationships. Those connections are what's going to make a real difference in your life and career.
- *Don't keep score.* Truly connecting with others is a constant process of giving and receiving—of asking for and offering help. You've got to be willing to be generous, and accept the generosity of others, without keeping tally.
- *Be audacious.* Nothing will create more opportunity in life than a willingness to step up and ask for what you need. It's that simple. Push beyond what you think is "allowed" and you'll often find that people are eager to help.

The Obstacle Is the Way: The Timeless Art of Turning Trials into Triumph
BY RYAN HOLIDAY

As the subtitle states, Holiday's book outlines how you can turn setbacks into successes. Holiday's advice is largely inspired by stoics, with Roman emperor Marcus Aurelius being the most influential. Here are three of my favorite passages:

- "Focusing exclusively on what is in our power magnifies and enhances our power. But every ounce of energy directed at things we can't actually influence is wasted…So much power…is frittered away in this manner."
- "It's supposed to be hard. Your first attempts aren't going to work. It's goings to take a lot out of you—but energy is an asset we can always find more of. It's a renewable resource."
- "See things for what they are. Do what we can. Endure and bear what we must. What blocked the path now is a path. What once impeded action advances action. The Obstacle is the Way."

Outliers: The Story of Success
BY MALCOLM GLADWELL

I highly recommend anything from Malcolm Gladwell, but *Outliers* is my favorite of his works. In this book, Gladwell tackles a popular topic: what makes high-achievers different? He argues that we focus too much on what successful people are like and not enough on intangible factors such as where they are from, when they were born, and unique opportunities they had. The 10,000 hour rule—the belief that it takes 10,000 hours of deep and dedicated practice to become an expert at something—is frequently referenced and stands as a reminder that it's not enough to just have talent or a high IQ.

The Power of Habit: Why We Do What We Do in Life and Business
BY CHARLES DUHIGG

Anyone who has tried to break a bad habit or start a new one knows how difficult it can be. Duhigg argues that understanding how habits work is the key to exercising regularly, losing weight, becoming more productive, building revolutionary companies and social movements, and achieving success.

He describes how they work in a three-step loop he calls *the habit loop:*

> "First, there is a cue, a trigger that tells your brain to go into automatic mode and which habit to use. Then there is the routine, which can be physical or mental or emotional. Finally, there is a reward…"

Learning how habits work has helped me develop new ones and avoid bad ones.

Smartcuts: How Hackers, Innovators, and Icons Accelerate Success

BY SHANE SNOW

In *Smartcuts*, author Shane Snow disproves the idea that climbing the ladder rung by rung is required if you want to reach the top. Instead, he argues that conventions like "paying dues" actually prevent progress, and that lateral thinking (solving problems through an indirect and creative approach) is how the most successful people have always made it. But, as Snow says, "Lateral thinking doesn't replace hard work; it eliminates unnecessary cycles." Snow's book is highly engaging and worth reading for anyone seeking to accelerate success in their career.

The Start-up of You

BY REID HOFFMAN AND BEN CASNOCHA

I described this book in Chapter 9, but I'll add a few additional takeaways here:

- Before dreaming about the future or making plans, you need to articulate what you already have going for you—as entrepreneurs do.
- No matter how brilliant your mind or strategy, if you're playing a solo game, you'll always lose out to a team. Building a strong network is critical.

- The fastest way to change is to surround yourself with people who are already the way you want to be.

Hoffman and Casnocha also co-wrote *The Alliance: Managing Talent in the Networked Age,* where they contend that the employer-employee relationship is broken. They believe the solution is to "stop thinking of employees as family or free agents, and start thinking of them as allies on a tour of duty."

Steve Jobs

BY WALTER ISAACSON

I didn't read Jobs' biography until a few years after it was published. Jobs is so frequently quoted and discussed in the business world that I doubted I'd find value from Isaacson's 600+ page account. I was wrong. Isaacson tells an incredible story of a creative, complex, innovative, and enigmatic man who sought to put a dent in the universe. I loved learning about Jobs' so-called "Reality Distortion Field" that allowed him to bend reality and convince others they could do the impossible. As Isaacson said:

> "[Jobs'] legacy is transforming seven industries: personal computers, animated movies, music, phones, tablet computing, digital publishing, and retail stores. His legacy is creating what became the most valuable company on earth, one that stood at the intersection of the humanities and technology, and is the company

most likely still to be doing that a generation from now. His legacy, as he said in his "Think Different" ad, was reminding us that the people who are crazy enough to think they can change the world are the ones who do."

The Talent Code
BY DANIEL COYLE

The Talent Code provides an articulate review of how to grow talent and maximize potential in yourself and others. Coyle's book is broken down into three sections, each one an important step in developing talent:

1) **Deep practice.** Engaging in deep practice isn't just going through the motions but instead requires operating on the edge of your ability. Slowing down and breaking the task into components is critical.

2) **Ignition.** To achieve deep practice over an extended period of time, you have to have deep passion. Without passion you won't have the motivation to stay with it.

3) **Master coaching.** Characteristics of master coaches include listening more than talking, giving immediate and highly specific feedback, and tailoring the feedback to the student's way of learning.

I loved learning about the Brazilian soccer players who elevated their talents by playing Futsal, an indoor five-on-five version of soccer played with a smaller, heavier ball on a tiny field. Futsal allowed these players to get five times the number of reps they'd normally get in a typical game. This enabled them to develop skills at an accelerated pace. The book inspired me to identify talents I want to develop and find ways to dramatically increase reps and expedite the learning process.

Unbroken: A World War II Story of Survival, Resilience, and Redemption

BY LAURA HILLENBRAND

Given the popularity of the book and movie, I hesitated including *Unbroken* on this list, but it's the best book I've ever read. Louis Zamperini lived an amazing life, and Hillenbrand has penned a wonderfully written biography.

Acknowledgments

First and foremost I need to give a big thank you to my brother, Jordan. He was the first to provide feedback on the initial drafts of each chapter and served as the perfect sounding board for my ideas. Additionally, this book would not be what it is without the help of Elise Caffee. Her substantive and developmental editing was invaluable.

I am also grateful to all of the following who shared ideas, commented on drafts, gave me encouragement and/or supported me in other ways: Boubacar Barry, Brenda George, Chase Weed, Dave Crosby, Devin Paul, Jacob Morris, James Markham, Julie Geilman Mitchell, Kim Smith, Liz Wiseman, Nate Meikle, Rob Callan, Scott Christofferson, and Troy Nielson.

Above all, thank you to my parents, Alison and Roland, for their continual love and support, and my wife Whitney, for being by my side through all of the ups and downs.

About the Author

Nathan Tanner is currently a graduate student at Brigham Young University working on a Master of Business Administration degree where he focuses on organizational behavior, human resources, and talent management.

Prior to business school, Nathan worked several years as an investment banker, advising high-growth technology companies, and as a financial advisor, managing the financial affairs of high-net worth individuals. Nathan is passionate about career management and has helped countless students and young professionals find jobs.

Nathan lives in Utah with his wife, Whitney, and their two children, but will be moving to the San Francisco Bay Area upon graduation.